THE
Musician'e
Advice for All Musicians, ofessional

BY PETER ERSKINE
& DAVE BLACK

Alfred Music
P.O. Box 10003
Van Nuys, CA 91410-0003
alfred.com

ISBN-10: 1-4706-4247-6
ISBN-13: 978-1-4706-4247-1

All photos and art, except author photo (p. 6)
and eyeball art (p. 25), are courtesy of Getty Images.

Contents

About the Authors

Peter Erskine has played the drums for sixty years. He appears on over 700 albums and film scores, has written 12 books, has won 2 GRAMMY Awards, and is the recipient of an Honorary Doctorate from Berklee College of Music. Over 50 albums have been released under his own name or as co-leader. He's played with Stan Kenton, Maynard Ferguson, Weather Report, Steps Ahead, Joni Mitchell, Steely Dan, Diana Krall, among others, and has appeared as a soloist with the Los Angeles, Chicago, London, Oslo, Helsinki, BBC, and Berlin Philharmonic Orchestras. Peter graduated from the Interlochen Arts Academy and studied with George Gaber at Indiana University. He is currently the Director of Drumset Studies at the University of Southern California, and continues to maintain a very active playing and recording career.

Dave Black received his Bachelor of Music in percussion performance from California State University, Northridge. A prolific composer and arranger, more than 60 of his compositions/arrangements have been published/recorded by several of the major music publishers. Many have been used as source/background music on numerous TV shows and movies, including the film *Drumline*. He is the recipient of numerous awards and commissions, including 26 consecutive ASCAP Popular Composer Awards, two GRAMMY participation/nomination certificates, the Percussive Arts Society President's Industry Award, a Modern Drummer Readers Poll award, two Drum! Magazine Drummie! awards, and a certified Gold Record award for the sale of more than 500,000 copies of *Alfred's Drum Method, Book 1*. As one of the biggest-selling percussion authors in the world, he is the author and/or co-author of over 30 books with combined sales now totaling over two million units.

Foreword

Why *The Musician's Lifeline?*

The initial impulse for writing this book was to build upon the success of our previous collaboration, *The Drummer's Lifeline: Quick Fixes, Hacks, and Tips of the Trade.* This book would represent our combined knowledge and opinions formed by lives lived in music. Since Dave and I are both drummers, we naturally felt that, while much of our advice would be universal in scope and appeal, we needed to bring another voice into the authorial mix. But who?

Turns out that we both had the same inspired thought one morning, and our emails—like ships crossing in the morning sun—were semaphoring the same message: "What if we invited the best musicians we can think of to participate?"

So, that's what we did. To our everlasting gratitude, over 150 of the best musicians and educators we have the honor of knowing agreed to answer this simple set of questions:

1. **What's the best advice you've ever received?**
2. **What's the best advice you've ever given?**
3. **What's the one thing you'd have done differently in your studies/career?**
4. **Best travel advice?**
5. **Best sight-reading advice?**
6. **Do you have any business advice for a musician?**
7. **Any advice relating to people skills?**

Plus, a bonus question for non-drummers—re: advice to a drummer, and a few more bon mots of wisdom regarding auditions, recording, etc.

The answers will surprise, inform, and confirm what you already know or completely contradict what you've been taught by others.

This is a book you can read straight through in one sitting or jump around willy-nilly if you like ... and always return to time and again. Our hope is that this book will become a trusted source and friend.

Herewith we give you *The Musician's Lifeline.*

Peter Erskine & Dave Black
Los Angeles, 2019

Acknowledgements
We would like to thank all of our contributing experts for their feedback and support. This book is so much the better because of your input.

Sample: Seven Questions & Answers

Below is an example of how Peter and Dave answered the questions.

1. What's the best advice you've ever received?

Peter: Always compose when you play.
Dave: Pursue what you love and not what you think will pay the most.

2. What's the best advice you've ever given?

Peter: Play what you'd like to hear.
Dave: Set a time frame to reach your goal, and then move on. Also, have a plan B in place.

3. What's the one thing you would have done differently in your studies or career?

Peter: I would have studied counterpoint in college.
Dave: I would have studied more piano.

4. Best travel advice?

Peter: Be good to the people who handle your bags and your food.
Dave: Make copies of your passport and important documents.

5. Best sight-reading advice?

Peter: Look ahead!
Dave: If you make a mistake, breathe, relax, and keep going.

6. Do you have any business advice for a musician?

Peter: Don't be afraid to say "No" to a gig.
Dave: Follow your own path, not the path of others.

7. Any advice relating to people skills?

Peter: Be kind to others, and do no harm.
Dave: Don't make assumptions.

We also invited our "panel" of experts to weigh in regarding the challenges of auditioning, as well as provide some advice to drummers.

The questionnaire was emailed to 250 persons, with 164 of them responding. In addition to these direct responses, we benefitted from a one-degree-of-separation-passing-along-of-wisdom from no less than Miles Davis, Tony Williams, Wayne Shorter, Ron Carter, Shelly Manne, and Henry Mancini by way of their sidemen, colleagues, and students. So, there's no shortage of advice and answers here! To be honest, these responses are an embarrassment of riches, each worthy of its own page.

Read on!

Dear Peter and Dave,
My answer is a synthesis to
all of your questions:

Practice, practice, practice!

Best of luck,
Lalo Schifrin

HOW TO PLAY BETTER

PROBLEM: How do I play better?

TIP: Listen to the music, and play what you'd like to hear...not what your hands, fingers, or lips know. Play what your ears and heart tell you to play. It's really that simple.

RULE: No licks! Compose when you play. Use your imagination, but always play for the song.

REASON: Job number one is to play in a way that makes all the other musicians play their best. Within this duty, there are an infinite number of choices we can make. Add to that the complicating factor or feeling of playing to someone else's expectations, ego satisfaction, audience response, and so on—this is when the muscles begin to take over the musical mind. The simplest solution? Just play what you'd like to hear, not necessarily what you'd like to play. Those can be two very different things. Experience brings the hearing and playing process together as one. And certainly don't play what you imagine someone *else* wants to hear. Not in jazz, at any rate.

That said, it's normally necessary to establish your credibility on the bandstand with the other musicians onstage, as well as those listening out front. Tone, musicality, time, and feel.

The correct playing of the melody is the "correct passcode" to gaining trust and acceptance when it comes to any style of music. If you fail at that, you'll have to claw your way back into that position of melodic and improvisational authority. It's not hard to do: it only takes the **commitment** and discipline to do it.

And, yes...
practice.

PROBLEM: Closed eyes

TIP: Practice playing with your eyes open. Look at the source of the music around you, and do not close your eyes or stare off into space. Connect. We're trying to have a conversation up here.

CONCEPT: No moving before you begin to play. **Internalize** the tempo, and **know** the time and feel; you're not going to help yourself by nodding your head and tapping your toes.

KNOW IT = OWN IT

We recommend telling your students to **stop moving their head** from side to side as if they're really digging what they're playing. Tell them to be more inscrutable, like the Sphinx. Not only do they look hipper and play better, they're also learning something about Greek mythology.

Or, as Clint Eastwood told me [Peter] (explaining his strong, silent type of character): "I hold a lot in, and let it out...a little at a time."

Concentrate!

Think of the time, and not what you might play. And, listen!

With time, you can play anything. Without time, nothing you play will matter.

And *save* the hip stuff when improvising...too much too soon and it has no impact after a very short while.

Speaking of hip stuff and time: it's important that you take the time and interest to learn the lyrics of the songs you are playing whenever possible. This will not only help you understand the feeling of the song, but it will enable you to play with **clarity, intention**, and **specificity**.

Freedom is said to come from discipline. Imposing your own creative discipline or restrictions can help you achieve your desired artistic outcome—that is, more freedom!

It takes courage, discipline, and giving yourself permission to be musical.

Encourage your students as follows: "It's good discipline to always maintain the high road, the high standard with anything and everything you practice or play, okay?"

Attitude

When you walk into any playing situation, one with friends or with complete strangers, project quiet confidence and command, because that's the gig.

That said, do your best to leave your ego at the door; make it about the music and not about how you think you sound or look to others.

Some additional advice:

- **Show up early for every gig, and be ready to go!**
- **Play what the music requires.**
- **Set up so you can have eye contact with the other musicians.**
- **Keep your instrument in good working condition.**
- **Stay healthy.**
- **Warm up.**

Warm-Ups

There is much to be said for the melding of the mind and body when we first encounter our instrument each day—a philosophy of biomechanics where the Zen rubber meets the road. We are taught that "practice makes perfect," and that every practice routine should include a warm-up session. But how many of us diligently warm up before practicing? How often do we sit down to play a concert or recording session without doing any sort of warm-up? One thing we do know is that the older we get, the more helpful and important warming up becomes. This is true for any instrumentalists (jazz, rock, funk, pop, or classical).

The biomechanical benefits of warming up are obvious. It is the spiritual side, however, that might not be so apparent. The warm-up session is a sort of benediction to your playing day. It is quiet time alone, with the tools of your trade and the silent musical space around you. This is music waiting to happen. This is the time to breathe deeply, and to feel the expression of gratitude for what you're about to do. As you codify and confirm your movements and execution, you are brought face to face with the very essence of being a musician. In essence, we think it in our minds, feel it in our souls, and say it with our sticks, mouthpieces, fingers, reeds, or bows.

QUESTION: How soon should I be set up and ready to play before the downbeat?

ANSWER: At least 15 minutes. As the saying goes, "If you're early you're on time, if you're on time you're late, and if you're late you're fired!" Give yourself plenty of time to get to the gig in case something goes wrong (a flat tire, wrong directions, an accident on the freeway, a lane closure, etc.), so you can be set up and ready to play between 15 to 30 minutes before the downbeat. Being early and relaxed lets the client and/or bandleader know you're a pro, and it helps contribute to the overall success of the gig. If it's a recording session, the norm is for everyone to be in the studio ready to go one hour before the downbeat.

PROBLEM: I'm recording, and this recording will be around forever.

SOLUTION: Relax. It's merely a snapshot. Hopefully your eyes aren't closed when the picture is taken. It's merely a moment in time. Just concentrate and have fun.

ADVICE: Don't forget to **breathe** when you play. Breathing not only makes all things possible, it will also help you to relax, and it will have a most positive effect on your musical phrasing. Also, **listen**.

QUESTION: How do I play with a click?

ANSWER: The best way to play to a click track (or metronome) is, of course, to play right with it. But the best **trick** is to "chase" the click instead of allowing yourself to somehow get ahead of it. Experienced studio musicians will most often opt to chase the click track. If you practice with a metronome, we do not recommend you set the click sound on beats 2 and 4, as this is never done in the studio. Learn to swing or play any feel with the metronome sounding on the beat. The more you do it, the more natural the process will become.

The click is your friend.

—New York studio guitarist
Steve Khan to Peter in 1977

QUESTION: What's the best way to overdub and layer parts?

ANSWER (Peter): The late, great Michael Brecker shared this tip with me years ago as we were overdubbing his saxophone parts for an ensemble/*tutti* horn part on a Steps Ahead album. Mike played his first part and then attempted to overdub it while listening to it as part of the playback track...makes perfect sense, right? But his timing was just the slightest bit "off" (and this is Michael Brecker we're talking about, who had some of the best time of any musician I've ever known). So, Mike asked that we turn off his first part in the headphone cue, whereupon he layered the 2nd and 3rd harmony parts in perfect rhythmic unison: timing, phrasing, *everything*. He told me that he learned this trick from the Bee Gees, who did all of their incredible harmony overdub work this way. Their memories were more effective than their ears and response times!

More Tricks of the Trade

"Be still my beating heart (and my bouncing leg)."

PROBLEM: My leg bounces too much for no good reason.

TIP: Stop it.

BACKGROUND (from Peter): When I was a member of the group Weather Report, founder, keyboardist, and leader Joe Zawinul once asked me to play a beat for him, and when I did he noticed that my left leg was bouncing up and down in rhythm even though it was not being used to play the (hi-hat) pedal. "What's going on with your leg?" he asked. "What do you mean? I'm just moving it in time..." "No," he interrupted, "Put that energy into what you are playing."

This is insanely good advice for any musician. It not only serves to focus your musical energy to where it needs to be going, it also ensures that you are internalizing the beat versus externalizing the beat. The time is not in our elbows or forearms, or thighs or legs...the time is in our minds and hearts, and the more relaxed our limbs are, the more quickly and smoothly we can respond to any and every whim of our creative imaginations.

Foot-Tapping

Some thoughts:

1. We're not a fan of foot-tapping on the bandstand or in the studio, for the primary reason that it makes noise! If you want or need to tap your toes, then develop a way to move them inside your footwear without manifesting an actual tap on the floor.

2. If you're going to tap, then pay attention to how often you're tapping. The old view/advice was to tap the foot on every quarter note, but jazz educator and theorist Hal Galper advises to tap on beats 1 and 3, as this creates a more swinging flow.

3. This taps into our own observations that music is felt or played best when the rate of the foot tap does not exceed the passage of four subdivisions. For example, a swung eighth-note jazz feel practically begs for the listener or musician to either snap their fingers on beats 2 and 4 or tap their toes on beats 1 and 3... while a funk tune by, say, Earth, Wind & Fire begs the listener to tap their toes on each quarter note or the space it takes for four sixteenth notes to occur. Tap your foot more than that, and you risk being a square.

So, the rule in rhythm section-based music: allow four subdivisions to go by between taps. *Our* rule, at any rate.

Please Be Seated...

Pay attention to how you sit. Are you sitting on your legs (thighs), or are you sitting on your "rockers" or "sit bones"?

Rotate your pelvis so your imaginary tail is sticking out at a 45-degree angle behind you and your chest is open to the world (and the music) with your shoulders pulled back and not hunched forward. Your body, mind, and soul will be more receptive to musical input, and your back will feel much better after any rehearsal, practice session, or gig.

Relax your shoulders. You're not going to swing if your body is tense.

PROBLEM: You're giving me a lot of good advice, but it's too much to think about when I'm playing!

TIP: Don't think. **Concentrate!**

> Practice is for the practice room. When you're in front of an audience, forget mechanics... relax, concentrate, and **create.**
>
> —**Bill Platt,** *principal percussionist of the Cincinnati Symphony Orchestra (40 years, now retired)*

Reading

CHALLENGE: Counting while reading

TIP: While we do not count while playing something notated on a page of music, we do count when needed to keep track of rests and how many bar numbers will pass before the next entrance. It's easy to lose track of the count—examples include film sessions where the music or onscreen action distracts you, or hearing one thing but seeing "another" in terms of the bar or the layout of the measures, etc. We suggest using your fingers and counting intently, with intention! It's okay to use your fingers to count—discreetly, of course. You can start with your thumb and then add each finger one measure at a time, touching the thumb with that finger until you reach "5," and then starting all over again ("6...7..." and so on). The tactile connection may help you keep score.

If you're working with a click track, that makes it relatively easy to know where the beat is; otherwise, be sure to keep an eye on the conductor while you're reading and/or counting!

The ability to read music is essential to being a complete musician. There is no reason for anyone to practice or promote illiteracy in any language, music included.

Peter: It is **not** necessary to learn how to read really complicated rhythms (with superimposed metric schemes, etc.), although it can't hurt, I guess...but, in all the years I've worked in the studio or with orchestras, big bands, and combos of every description, most of the time I've only had to deal with eighth notes, quarter notes, plus some sixteenths and triplets here and there. Quintuplets or groupings of seven over nine, etc.? Only once in a dream about Frank Zappa's music.

That said, I pride myself on being able to read basic note values quickly and reliably in just about any combination. How did I learn to do this? I practiced reading every day and worked towards speed-reading of basic note values, etc.

TIP: Sing as you play.

Otherwise, just figure out the subdivisions. As one of the BBC Symphony percussionists explained to me when I asked her how it was possible to play the über-complicated rhythms of Olivier Messiaen's *Chronochromie*, she cheerfully replied, "Oh, it's just all 2s and 3s..."

TRICK: If and when you encounter a measure of music with a gobbledy-gook of rests in the middle, scan forward to the **end** of the measure and read backwards (all while you're reading forward). We know...it sounds complicated...but it's not. You can very quickly determine that the next note you'll need to play is, for example, on the "+" of beat 3, and you won't have to guess what all of those rests add up to. We refer to this as check-sum reading.

Basic note values and their relative lengths (duration) are simple math. And, just like math, the numbers do not lie. Whatever the time signature, the notes must (and will) add up correctly.

TIP: Get yourself a copy of the Louie Bellson/Gil Breines book *Modern Reading Text in $\frac{4}{4}$ for All Instruments*, and spend ten minutes a day reading it. You will become a better reader before you know it. As I told one of my students: "You need to be able to read this stuff like you're drinking water." Suggested practice routine: 15 minutes a day challenging yourself with the Bellson book until you can eat those rhythms, play them in your sleep, etc. This reading is not so much a conscious choice but an automatic response to the visual information on the page, allowing you to make music from it versus struggling with it. No one is interested in, "Oh, sorry...wait."

Sight-Reading Advice from the Pros

There is no secret to sight-reading.
The more you do it, the better you get at it.

—*Gary Burton*

Listen as you read, and know the form or road map.—*Steve Fidyk*

Focus, look ahead, and listen deeply, like you wrote the music.
—*John Daversa*

Train your eyes to divide the bar and look for patterns.—*Janis Siegel*

1. Practice with a metronome.

2. Do not stop no matter how many mistakes you might make (by not stopping you are training your eyes to read ahead).

Read phrases, not just the notes.
—*Gary Hobbs*

3. Sight-read everything you can, including music for instruments other than your own.—*Tom Ranier*

Make it a part of your daily practice.—*Alan Pasqua*

Circle all repeat signs.—*Scott Goodman*

Study the piece before trying to play through it.—*Joe Lovano*

Stay with the pulse, let go of mistakes, and don't stop or hesitate.—*Su-a Lee*

When you're first handed a chart, use those 30 seconds before the count-off to scan the whole part from start to finish.—*John Goldsby*

Read two bars ahead.
—Cecilia Tsan

Always look a measure ahead.—*John Beck*

1. Slow it down.

2. Look left-right-left and scan. Look at the left-hand corner for time signature, tempo, style, dynamics, and other details. Look at the right-hand corner (the end) to see how it ends—short, long, fermata, softly, coda, etc. Now, go back to the beginning and quickly scan through the entire piece, making mental notes about repeat signs, the D.S., where it goes to the coda, solos, etc.

—*John Clayton*

Follow the shape of the line. Look ahead and let things go.—Alexa Tarantino

> **Always read ahead, at least a bar or two, especially at the end of staves.**—*Bill Platt*

In your private practice time, set the tempo, a metronome, where it is comfortable for *you*. Try to practice reading so you get the feeling that you are doing well at it. Don't set yourself up to fail or to be disappointed.

—*Steve Khan*

Don't stop. Just read. Then go back and look at your mistakes. You can't stop in real life so don't stop the first time you look at a piece of music. It will actually increase your confidence and teach you to naturally look ahead and "see" sentences and phrases better.—*Vinnie Colaiuta*

Do it! Keep your chops up.
—*Leland Sklar*

Sight-read things without stopping, no matter what happens. Group sight-reading practice = it's more fun with more people. Do it!
—Dale Hikawa Silverman

Look for patterns.

Everything repeats.

—Ethan Iverson

Mistakes will happen; how you recover and persevere is crucial. Stay on the bus, or at least try to get back on the bus as soon as possible. —Fred Simon

Find the hardest passages first and shed them. —Nathan East

To quote the great **Elvin Jones, "Get a light for your music stand!"**
—John DeChristopher

Always look ahead of where you are. You only "sight-read" something once. After that it's no longer sight-reading.
—Carl Allen

Learn to move your eyes forward—read from the back of the bar, which will make more sense to the front of the bar if it seems difficult.—Rick Kvistad

Sight-read every day. Any music, any instrument, any sort of notation, in different directions on the paper.—Claus Hessler

This skill takes maintenance. Read something every day. Stay relaxed, and always look ahead so you're not surprised by what's coming. Look at the road map ahead of time, note the general range of written lines, and don't forget to play naturally. Interpret musically as you read the notes.—Damian Erskine

A musician will only sight-read well if he or she spends time sight-reading (experience); good athletes have spent time being athletic (experience), good boxers have spent time boxing (experience), and good singers have spent time singing (experience). Anything done well is because of experience doing it at all levels.—*Chuck Rainey*

Read a number of new pieces every day. The only way to be good at sight-reading is to practice sight-reading. Think of it like developing specific muscles you use only for specific things. You can only develop them by using them. The more you sight-read in the practice room, the better you'll sight-read in your ensemble.
—*Marvin Stamm*

FULLY
FOCUS

on reading the chart, and learn as much as possible in the first run-through. Believe it or not, you remember more than you think, making the second reading that much easier.—*Ralph Humphrey*

Do it all the time.—*George Garzone*

Practice rhythm and ear-training daily. If you don't live, feel, and hear the notes you see, then the reading won't work.—Ingrid Jensen

Do it often, and always read ahead.—*Jiggs Whigham*

Of course, look ahead, especially for clumps of accidentals (and anticipate the overall sense of tonal flow).—*Otmaro Ruíz*

Learn how to tap out the rhythms. Familiarize yourself with them. They're your friends. They never change, and once you learn them, you know them. Knowing them allows you to focus on the pitches.—*Will Lee*

Scan in advance for tricky bits; try to be as musical as possible.—William Kanengiser

Rests *are musical notes that dictate duration.*
Music is in the science sometimes; play the rest(s)...
look ahead, and count!—*Ivan Hampden, Jr.*

Understanding structure helps eliminate reading note to note. When you have a passage that is over an altered dominant chord, it's likely that there are going to be a lot of accidentals—figure out the scale form. Reading feels very similar to improvisation to me—it's all related to having a strong sense of musical architecture.
—*Larry Koonse*

and trust yourself. If you're not good at it, it's like everything else—**practice!**—*Neil Percy*

Don't forget to make it sound wonderful.—*Ed Carroll*

Arrive early.
—*Dan Carlin*

Work on transcribing recorded solos—even just the rhythms of a recorded solo or of a big-band shout section. You're using the same "muscles." When transcribing, you hear performed music, visualize the notation, and write it down. When you sight-read, you see the notation, envision (pre-hear) the sound, and perform the music. They're each the same process in reverse order.
—*Antonio García*

Do it as often as possible! Even if you just read eight bars every day.—*Christian McBride*

Sight-read often! Do some transposing in your sight-reading. Look at transposed scores while listening to music.—*Bob Mintzer*

Practice sight-reading all styles of music daily. Recognize style, repeated patterns, chord progressions, musical structure, and the "road map" quickly.
—Julie Berghofer

I am always glad that I started on piano to understand notation and clefs. My advice to musicians who play any other instrument: learn the basics of playing piano, as it will help you read and comprehend music for your entire career.
—Chris Brubeck

Don't forget to use your ears along with your eyes. —Glenn Kotche

Quiet all the mental dialogue so you can hear what you're seeing, and then trust yourself. —Liesl Whitaker

Keep your ears open! —Ed Soph

Look at the big picture. —Adam Nussbaum

Don't be afraid to wear glasses.
—Marty Panzer

Make sure you have all pages of the chart and they are in order! —Bill Cunliffe

WHY is this such a mystery for some musicians? Reading music is a language like any other. Learn the grammar and it will serve you well. It's simply a matter of being able to quickly recognize the patterns and symbols on the page, just as you are right now as you read this sentence. And if you buy into the philosophy that some musicians express, which says that reading music will detract from your individuality, then you are kidding yourself and are just afraid to do the work. And really, it's not even THAT much work to become a good reader! Get to it and check that box! —**Gordon Goodwin**

Practice simple rhythms at extremely fast tempi.—*Jake Reed*

Read ahead of yourself—it works!—*John Scofield*

Advice for my younger pupils to take a deep breath, put their hands lightly on the steering wheel, and imagine that they are driving through a strange city, keeping sight of all speed limits, stop lights, road signs, and instructions well in advance. —*Pamela Havenith*

I actually love sight-reading! Always look ahead—this gives you a split second to prepare your fingers/bow to make creative choices that can work. Practicing sight-reading is always helpful, too! —*Alyssa Park*

PLAY DUETS WITH SOMEONE A LOT BETTER THAN YOU WHO HAS ZERO PATIENCE. —*Abbie Conant*

Top sight-readers are musicians who come closest, the first time, to getting not only the pitches, notes, and rhythms, but the feel, style, phrasing, articulation, flow, musical line, and dynamics, as well. The complete musical picture! —*Justin DiCioccio*

Keep on going, no matter what!
—*Joanne Pearce Martin*

Understand that sight-reading is an entirely different brain function for singers than for instrumentalists. For the latter, they (in effect) push a button to get the right note—so hand-eye coordination is key. For singers, the pitch must be grabbed out of thin air. So developing a strong sense of "perfect pitch" is a goal worth aspiring to. As far as rhythm goes, like percussionists, there is no substitute for practice. Singers should sight read a new piece of contemporary vocal music with challenging rhythms each and every day.—*Lynn Helding*

CHALLENGE (Over-the-Bar Phrasing): Okay, so you're reading a piece of music, and you come across the following metric scheme: one bar of $\frac{3}{4}$, followed by a bar of $\frac{3}{8}$, then a $\frac{2}{4}$ measure, followed by another bar of $\frac{3}{4}$, then $\frac{3}{8}$ and, finally, good ol' $\frac{4}{4}$. What do you do?

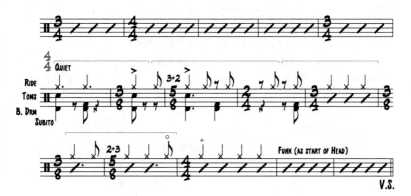

ANSWER (from Peter): There's no shame in graphing a metric scheme above the notated bars of music and using the accent scheme to help determine the strong (or "hip") parts of the overall beat or feel. In the example above, the seven bars of changing meters convert nicely into three bars of $\frac{4}{4}$ time! The music can be played in a way that feels good rather than forced.

When I pointed out this unnecessary challenge (yet pleasant anomaly) to composer Mark-Anthony Turnage, he merely replied, "Oh, yeah. Sorry." This solution reminds me of how my father used to drive his car on winding roads. Traffic allowing, he would "straighten out the road," doing less curves and more straight driving as conditions allowed. Not a bad idea to figure out the horizon line of any piece of music. It will not only feel better, but it will also make you less crazy in the end.

And it's always okay to write anything helpful onto a piece of music, *as long as you do it in pencil.*

Playing a Difficult Piece of Music

Before any concert where you'll need to really be on your toes in terms of playing in/leading/supporting the ensemble and music that involves a lot of reading and/or other challenges, find a quiet spot where you can sit and visualize the music before the performance, much like a downhill skier will visualize the race course before his or her ski run. By doing this, you'll know the turns and where the bumps are—by the time you get out there, you'll be able to enjoy the fresh air of the concert hall (the scenery, if you will) while feeling calm and completely focused on the task at hand. Don't avoid it—embrace it, and, in this way, you'll return as close as possible to your original state of music-making wonder, playing music for the sheer joy it brings. Your mind is clear—empty of distracting thoughts or concerns like ego, fear—free to swirl between each note and celebrate this most human of heavenly activities: making music.

It is possible to jinx a performance by injecting mention (a thought, a joke, whatever) of there being a problem or issue with the impending performance. FULL STOP. Don't do it. *Always* project a positive image in your own psyche. Visualize your success.

On a more practical note, if you're faced with playing a series of sixteenth-note offbeats and find the syncopation daunting, consider this: if you moved those sixteenth notes "over" by a sixteenth, then you'd simply be playing a series of eighth notes *on* the beat. What's hard about that? Nothing! Same for syncopations or offbeats. It's all music.

Sixteenth-Note Offbeat Rhythm

Sixteenth Notes on the Beat

Is Versatility Important?

Peter: Play the music you love—that's why we're all here in the first place! But, have an understanding and appreciation for as many other styles as possible. The great composer/arranger Johnny Richards kneeled down to me when I was a nine-year-old kid at a summer jazz camp, grabbed me by both shoulders, and implored me, while gazing into my eyes: "Peter, you be sure to listen to every kind of music."

Now, I'm not the world's foremost authority on reggae, but I've listened to it enough to play it convincingly for a song or two on a gig. Same goes for calypso. Funk. Polkas. Punk. Okay, not punk.

When you're an explorer, you never know what you might discover.

CHALLENGE: I am not from Brazil, so how do I play samba?

TIP: In addition to listening to samba, bossa nova, or *any* style of music you might want to play, there are secrets to phrasing, as well as rhythmic interpretation that will make your life easier. Think of samba in 2, not in 4.

Here's an exercise to help you hear and develop that delightful and unique "bump" in Brazilian music. Play the following rhythm by patting the sixteenth notes on your right thigh, and the eighth-note triplets on your left thigh:

While most of the forward motion of rhythm in most music can be thought of as a ball rolling down an incline, think of Brazilian music as being more like an egg rolling down that same incline.

Percussive Perspective

Rests and spaces are some of the most effective notes you'll ever use (not play!), but you *must* respect their full value and always be aware of the subdivisions going on in any piece of music. It's hard to create tension and release if you're not consistent or certain what the primary subdivision or feel actually is—we need to guide the listeners, too. We are **story tellers**, and we can't be full of baloney (to put it politely).

Think **horizontally** and the music will flow, and everyone can have a good time. Pun intended.

Make it dance.

Play the notes between the notes—silently.

And think of the backbeat as being long (L-o-o-o-n-g).

Chops? Here's a challenge for your students: If you can make a band swing (or rock or groove or whatever) with one hand only, then you can swing or groove *anything*. This is playing with **intention**. This is playing with fire. Pun intended.

And, enjoy the experience! Making music should not be like getting a tooth drilled at the dentist's office. The more you practice and prepare, the more everyone can enjoy the musical moment.

When it comes to drummers: Do drummers need to know music theory, too?

ANSWER: While there are some famous drummers who can't read music, they are the exception and not the rule. The very best drummers are those that have some background in music theory. Studying a melodic instrument, such as a piano or mallets, will give you a valuable understanding of harmony, chord structure, etc. You need to know about song forms before you can navigate through a chart, or to even play a tune without reading a chart. You must be able to visualize the form in your head. Hearing and recognizing harmonic function helps!

Quick! You're playing Duke Ellington's "Take the A Train," and the band stops at the bridge of the tune for you to play a short break or solo. How many bars do you play?✳

Knowing harmony and form makes it easier to recognize and play melodies at the drums. You know those big spaces between some notes of a drum solo? Learn to trust the music enough to give those long notes the intentional weight (not **loud**, but the weight of **intent**) to "sell" them to the listener.

And, don't worry about always trying to make your drumming interesting. Just focus on making it real.

PROBLEM: I'm playing conscientiously with good dynamics, but my drums sound **too loud** in the audience. What am I doing wrong? (Substitute "I'm" with "My drummer" if applicable.)

SOLUTION: Try to avoid snare hits that combine the rim with the drumhead! Drummers do this far more often than they realize, and while this can be a terrific way to get a cracking backbeat sound on the snare drum, it is overused to poor effect when accents are played. This combined sound of the rim plus head takes up more sonic space than you might expect, and in a "live" room or hall, the resulting sound is deadly to the music. It sounds like noise, so stop it.

When it comes to singers: What is the correct tempo when working with a singer?

ANSWER: Any tempo the singer wants!

Seriously! Vocalists must not only pay attention to pronunciation but hitting the notes as well—so if the tempo is wrong, no one is happy. Keep your eyes and ears open, as it's better to adjust the tempo to the singer's preference rather than fight and/or allow them to struggle through the delivery of the entire song. Remember, they're telling a story up there. Whether that story ends happily ever after or not could depend on you. A metronome will come in handy to note the "correct" tempo for a song, but this is always subject to change. Keep your eyes and ears open.

And, whatever instrument you play, make certain that your accompaniment never covers or obscures the lyrics.

What's the best way to approach double-time tempi or changes in the feel of the music?

Peter: I approach all music by visualizing or hearing multiple layers of time—much like a three-dimensional chessboard—incorporating:

1. **The primary pulse**

2. **The triplet subdivision**

3. **The vertical eighth-note subdivision (straight eighth)**

4. **Double time**

This allows or enables me to pivot to *any* level of the time without so much as a hiccup. This helps me to be aware of the music on a cellular level. All levels of time. All levels of dynamic(s). All levels of touch, tone, sound, propulsion, velocity, forward motion, and e-motion. The "Jedi-mind-trick" is to be aware of all of the musical elements and to *not* let the music rush you.

Esthetics

Is it just the fact that we were young when we discovered and listened so much to our heroes and mentors, etc., or is there a timeless strength to their music-making (like Picasso and art)? How do we approach this mountain of magnificence in order to attempt to climb it and plant our own flag?

QUESTION: How do I play more "modern"?

ANSWER: More modern doesn't equate to playing busier or louder! Whatever you do, you don't want your playing to tire the listener or other musicians out. Be creative without being overbearing, conversant without shouting, etc. **Think texture.**

Modernity in improvisation doesn't necessarily mean busier. Its meaning is closer to that of stretching the fabric of the time by **committing** to thematic ideas and rhythmic motivic development—evocation by provocation! Here are some things to keep in mind:

- Practice **modernity** while remaining musical.

- Don't equate **modern** with **too much**.

- **Tell the story**.

- Who's modern? Not as many people as they think they are.

- Whatever style of music you're playing (modern, classic, neo, or retro), tonal and textural balance, and contrast ratios need to have an esthetic clarity and beauty.

- Don't be afraid to let the car slip into fifth gear and cruise for a minute. Simmer, swing, and make the music bubble and dance.

Sometimes you can build more tension into a piece by playing simply and not always trying to be creative.

Make the Most of Your Playing

QUESTION: What's the best way to practice?

ANSWER: For starters, you can think of practicing in two ways: one, to get as much playing time under your belt as possible, and, two, to focus on specific items or to practice with intent.

Practicing for practicing's sake will help you build endurance and strengthen some coordinative motor skills, but the downside is that you're most often playing what you already know—*unless* you use this "free" time to truly pay attention to your accuracy and consistency in execution. In other words, it's a good idea to learn how to intuit what a particular piece of music is "telling" you to practice. **Listen** while you work.

Most musicians tend to practice the same things at the same tempos, over and over. And they practice what they know. We recommend practicing what you don't know. A journal will help keep track of what you've worked on. If you hit a wall? Stop, take a break, and move on to something else for a change of pace. You can and should return to the challenge that was frustrating you with a clear mind and spirit. It is possible to accomplish much more in 20 minutes of concentrated practice time than jamming for two hours on your instrument.

A mirror or video device is essential. Not only can you listen back to what you're playing (checking for dynamic balance, for example), you can play along with yourself to see and feel how the other musicians on the bandstand hear your playing. This is a real ear-opener. Unintentional cheating of the beat, etc., will immediately become apparent. The mirror or video will also reveal how much you are **externalizing** the beat versus **internalizing** the beat and playing with the most control.

More Practice Tips

- Make sure your equipment is working for you and not against you. If you're experiencing pain while practicing/playing, look into the reason why, and make the necessary fixes and/or adjustments.

- Spend time warming up at the beginning of each practice session to get your blood flowing and your body functioning smoothly and efficiently. Nonmusical warm-ups may include walking, running, or a variety of calisthenics.

- One of the most important roles of any musician is to play and/or sing in good time. Learning to practice with either a metronome, a drum machine, or a computer with music-sequencing software will help you to achieve this.

- Start slowly. Practice each rhythm or exercise at a comfortable, consistent tempo before increasing the speed.

- Master the awkward and uncomfortable, and make music out of *everything*.

- Count aloud, and either clap or sing each rhythm before playing. Don't move on until you can play what you're practicing at an equal volume and tempo throughout.

- Maintain a relaxed feel while playing, and breathe normally (breathing and relaxation are very crucial elements).

- Listen to the sound you're getting, and strive to get the best tone from your instrument. It's not just mechanics. It's **tone**.

- Strive for proper balance. Are all the notes even and in time?

- As you practice, use a mirror to observe your hands, embouchure, and posture.

- Sing or tap the rhythms before attempting to play them.

- Try to look for any bad habits (your teacher or your own observations should point these out).

- Focus! When you're concentrating fully, things become more ingrained in your mind, making them easier to recall later.

- Experiment with rhythms and patterns that you create.

- Set new goals for yourself.

- Consistent practice is important in order to keep your body in good condition and to get the most from your practice sessions.

- Actively listen to a variety of musical styles, as this is one of the best learning tools available.

- If you don't have a band to play with regularly, use a play-along app or tracks.

- Keep a practice diary or log, and annotate or chronicle what you work on each day, and at which tempos.

- Always practice and play musically.

- Record yourself.

- Reward yourself!

- Enjoy practicing. Playing an instrument or singing is fun, and regular practice sessions will make you a better player.

Peter's Best Practice Tip

Play in tempo and record yourself—then, while listening back, play "body percussion" along with your recorded performance. By this I mean play a steady pattern using both hands on your thighs or torso: if and when the tempo shifts even the slightest bit, you'll feel it instantly—and you will gain an immediate sensation of how your time feel feels to other musicians.

The best practice advice Peter has ever read:

For classical musicians like myself, there can be such a thing as too much practice. We face labyrinths of notes, and our initial focus on the first day (or weeks) is on executing them with precision and fluidity. That close-up work on learning every note is necessary, but the language of the music is discernible only by stepping away to experience the monument rather than the bricks—the poetry rather than the letters that constitute it. My favorite part of the process is when I can reverse my inside-out approach and take it all in, often by stepping away from the piano.—*Gloria Cheng*

Know the feel.
Know your subdivisions.
DON'T GUESS!

AUDITIONS

Preparing for an Audition—
Part One, for a Professional Job

Where Can I Find a List of Available Auditions?

1. Check orchestra or local musician union websites for any job and/or audition postings. You can also check AFM magazines and third-party websites such as "Musical Chairs" and "Audition Café."

2. If there's a performance organization in a particular city or region of the world you would like to live, periodically check the websites of those performance organizations.

3. Before taking an audition, we suggest you do a little research on the group/ensemble you will be auditioning for. This can include listening to their recordings or attending concerts in order to get a better understanding of how they perform as a unit.

4. Once you know the dates of the audition, start looking for travel and lodging accommodations so you'll know what the costs are up front in order to know what you have to save.

Applying for an Audition

In many cases, orchestras will usually ask for a one-page resume/CV that should include your education history, professional experience, and references. These resumes are screened about 75 percent of the time, and the candidates are either rejected or invited to audition. In some cases, they may also ask for a prescreened audition video or audio recording to be submitted. If you pass their qualifications in both areas, you will most likely be asked to audition in the first round.

If the Audition Is Out of Town, Who Is Responsible for the Cost Related to Travel and Accommodations?

Usually the person auditioning is responsible for the cost related to travel and accommodations. In some cases, such as military bands like the President's Own, Pershing's Own, etc., travel and/or accommodation expenses may be covered if you're invited to a live, final round.

> Do a lot of thinking as far as which suitcases work best with gear and how to transport gear and instruments from the hotel to the venue without destroying your arms. Other than that, pack light, and book a cheap flight.—*Matt Howard*

Preparing for the Audition

1. Once you know your audition date, write it on your calendar and work backwards to calculate how long you have to prepare for it. Make a detailed plan for every week leading up to the audition so you can achieve the best results without wasting time.

2. Find out what excerpts/pieces are required, and get them in your hands as quickly as possible. Once you've mastered the technical aspects of a piece, you can start to work on musicality.

3. When preparing orchestral excerpts, listen to how other orchestras have performed them, and try to incorporate some of your own interpretations without deviating too far from the integrity of the music.

4. Record yourself so you can hear if your ideas are coming across clearly.

5. Consider playing mock auditions for colleagues, family, and friends to help you deal with nervous energy.

6. If the audition material is your choice, choose a piece(s) you know well and are comfortable with. The idea is to do well on your audition, so try to avoid impressing the panel by choosing a piece that is too difficult or that you don't feel comfortable playing.

7. Always have backup pieces ready. It's not unusual to be asked to play something else, and you'll need to be ready.

8. Make sure you know whether you will be expected to do aural tests and/or sight-reading in your audition.

9. If there is a planned interview in addition to a performance audition, make sure you prepare some answers in advance.

10. If you know someone who has auditioned in the past, ask him or her what sort of questions to expect. This will help you become more prepared and confident.

11. Work on being able to perform the excerpts in almost any situation. In the last couple weeks leading up to the audition, consider performing the whole list once or twice a day. Ideally you should be able to perform the list when you're tired, stressed, or alert, as you never know what unexpected things you'll run into on the day of the audition.

12. Before an audition, prepare mentally by meditating, reading books on additional subject matter that's of interest, or removing yourself from social media.

13. You have to believe in yourself more than anyone else.

Be prepared—know why you are there and what the job entails, and do your very best.—*Bernard "Pretty" Purdie*

Because it's just that—an audition to play alongside professionals—but few consider the intangibles. Something will go wrong, or you will be asked to play a passage differently. Have you considered how you will react and respond? Inspire.

—*Ed Carroll*

Auditions can be tricky, because often there is a lot riding on them. But if you can get into a mindset that says, "I am playing music, and it doesn't matter if I am in my bedroom, in the school band room, or onstage at the Hollywood Bowl. It is the same process. I don't think about who is in the audience, what is at stake due to the performance, or how much I am (or am not) getting paid. It's about the music, and I will not pollute that experience with those peripheral distractions!" Music is too important to not give it your 100-percent commitment. Achieving this mindset is easier said than done, but if you keep reminding yourself about the concept, and keep breathing in order to dissipate your tension, you can get there.—*Gordon Goodwin*

On the classical side, my teacher advised me to collect challenging orchestral excerpts together in a folder and practice them regularly, so that I would be prepared for last-minute auditions. She also required certain cadenzas, solo passages, etc. to be memorized.

—*Julie Berghofer*

Sometimes you just have to play nervous!

—*John Scofield*

Try to relax!—*Fred Simon*

Find a good and well-respected teacher to guide you. Be prepared by knowing the music cold. Listen to recordings of the works on the audition. Do as many mock auditions as you can to prepare you for the real audition.—*Raynor Carroll*

Be totally prepared, 150 percent prepared! Because nerves will melt away 50 percent of your preparation. Your motor skills should be infallible.—*Dale Hikawa Silverman*   Do as many "mock" auditions as you can, and not just immediately before the actual audition, but at least a month before. Gather together folks who make you nervous, and have them request your excerpts at random. Also, if you are performing a solo piece with piano as part of the audition, have your pianist play with you in the mock audition, if possible. Basically, do anything you can to duplicate the audition experience, preferably outside the comfort of your own home. And when the day comes, remember to let your musicianship shine through, even as you attempt to play everything perfectly. Remember why you started doing all this in the first place—*the music.*—*Joanne Pearce Martin*

For those winning auditions, the time to negotiate is before you sign a contract. After that they've got you!
—*Rick Kvistad*

Preparing for an Audition—
Part Two, for School

Here's a secret from the TV, film, and theatrical worlds when it comes to auditions: the people you're playing for are not looking for you to fail. In fact, they are hoping for you to succeed! A successful audition solves everyone's problems when it comes to choosing and casting. So, the first thing to remember is that the auditioning panel is really on your side.

Now, that being said, no one has ever left an audition thinking, "Wow, that's the best I've ever played, and that was easily the most fun I've ever had." Auditions to get into a school or get a place in an ensemble can be daunting affairs. Secret #2: The auditioning person or panel is not really looking to be impressed. Touch, tone, and basic musicality will always win the day. How well does the musician listen to the other players? What is his or her (musical and stylistic) vocabulary? How does he or she *sound*? Notice we did not include, "How well does he or she play?"

An audition is your introduction to someone. When you meet that person, look into his or her eyes when you say hello, and allow the person's honesty to speak to you. Big words and fancy language, whether spoken or played, don't necessarily make the best impression. Confidence comes from preparation. And *you* know yourself better than anyone else. If you've practiced, you should have nothing to worry about, and you should feel pretty good about going in and making some music.

Practice, listen, and have fun in life.

> Know your strengths, but try not to oversell them. Try to present an honest picture of yourself and how serious and dedicated you are to your craft. Like Bill Evans [pianist] said, "Take care of the music, and the rest will take care of itself."—*Aaron Serfaty*

The Day of the Audition

1. Make sure you get a good night's sleep the night before the audition.

2. Eat a good breakfast, as this will give you the energy needed to help get you started.

3. Find out what time you have to be at the location of your audition so you can plan your expected route, as well as the time you'll need to leave. If you are traveling by bus or car, allow extra time in case of traffic. If taking a train or bus, check online schedules for delays and/or cancellations.

4. Plan to arrive at the audition a little earlier than expected.

5. Don't over practice or spend your entire warm-up time practicing your audition material. We suggest you start by playing slow scales and/or a short exercise to help keep your mind off the audition.

6. Remember to do your best and not worry about the outcome. Think of the audition as a private performance you're giving to a few friends/colleagues. This will help you stay calm.

7. In order to stay relaxed, incorporate breathing exercises, walking, thinking about things not related to the audition, or any other methods you've developed over time.

8. Appear confident to the panel, even if you don't feel confident. When you walk in, give them a smile, and calmly answer any questions they may ask.

9. At the end of the audition, thank the panel before you leave, as you want to leave a good impression.

After the Audition

Don't dwell on or overanalyze your audition after it's finished. No matter how much you overthink or overanalyze your performance, you can't change anything after the fact.

College Auditions Advice from John Tafoya

Do the Obvious: Repertoire Requirements

Each college audition will require somewhat similar repertoire. However, make sure you have your repertoire requirements determined for each school. Most students will create a folder including copies of the planned repertoire along with a cover sheet (your name and then the planned solo repertoire listed).

Sight-Reading

Schools will list it but may or may not ask for it. Be ready to sight-read. Practice sight-reading daily. Take your time—slower, with more correct notes, is better—and be sure to keep playing in a steady tempo (catching phrasing and dynamics is a plus).

Interview

Be prepared. The most "basic" question may stump you—for example, "Why this school?" Any hesitation could really sway the professor's final evaluation. Study up on the school, faculty, ensemble experience, etc. Each school *should* have a detailed website. Do your homework and, most importantly, have questions for the faculty!

Have your mallets, sticks [instrument], and music ready to go.

It is customary to have a notebook ready (for each professor) that contains copies of your audition repertoire. Percussionists: Make sure that your preferred mallets are ready to go (remove all plastic bags, etc.)—you want to make the most of the time you have during your audition. Don't waste it!

Tuning Fork [for Timpani Players]

Yes, purchase an A=440 tuning fork to use when tuning the timpani. Running over to hit a note on the marimba or vibraphone is "OK," but it's much better to have your tuning fork ready to go. Get rid of the pitch pipes!

John Tafoya
Chairman, Percussion Department
Professor of Music
Indiana University Jacobs School of Music

SECTION 4 : **PERFORMANCE TIPS**

How to Deal with Performance Anxiety

Most people experience some type of performance anxiety, whether it's getting up in front a group of people to do a speech, play an instrument, sing, act, perform magic, participate in an athletic event, etc. Anxiety can manifest itself in many different ways including shortness of breath, a rapid heartbeat, dry mouth, shaky hands (voice, legs, and arms), cold or clammy hands, feeling sick to your stomach, etc. Anxiety can sometimes be so debilitating that it can prevent some from being able to pursue what they enjoy or even a particular career. Because performance anxiety is so common, we'd like to offer some easy tips to help get you through those stressful situations.

1. Acknowledge that it's natural to have performance anxiety.

2. Accept yourself for who you are.

3. Don't feel like you have to prove yourself to others.

4. Be prepared.

5. Limit caffeine and sugar intake.

6. Focus on the enjoyment you're providing others.

7. Don't focus on what could go wrong.

8. Try some relaxation techniques such as meditation, controlled breathing, taking a walk, exercise, eating healthy, shaking out your muscles, etc.

9. Laughter is a great way to deal with stress. So, read a funny book, or watch a funny movie or TV show.

10. Before an actual performance, play for your family and/or friends so you become comfortable performing in front of people.

There are less extreme types of reaction to anxiety, and those may include a level of self-consciousness that prohibits the kind of unfettered creative response to what the musician is hearing as he or she performs (whether as part of an ensemble or in a solo setting) that makes music-making fun. (We sound or play our best when we're having fun.) It might be helpful to remember this: no matter what someone is thinking about *your* performance, it does not actually change anything about the way *you* sound. The listener might love it, they might hate it, or they might be completely indifferent to it...none of those reactions have anything to do with the sound you are making or the rhythms you are playing. Only *your* reaction can affect the way you sound. So, when the going gets tough, the tough are best advised to laugh a little, take a deep breath, and then concentrate on the task at hand.

By the way: in our experience, the most potent form of anxiety is produced because the performer knows on some level that he or she did not prepare well enough for the task at hand. So, to go back to maestro Lalo Schifrin's advice: "practice"! Trust us—you'll be glad you did.

Manners

PROBLEM: Talk, talk, talk, talk.

TIP: The less said, the better.

BACKGROUND (from Peter): Many years ago, when I was first starting out in the New York City studio scene, I found myself in a studio recording music for a new television program. The producer of the program was fairly well known, and the composer/producer of the session was a gentleman I had worked with briefly/previously in Los Angeles. I'm not sure why, but I was "feeling my oats" during this evening session—I was rambunctious, loud-mouthed and, looking back, acting like a jerk. The session seemed to go well, musically. Imagine my shock the following morning when I received a telephone call from the composer, who rang me simply to tell me that my "bullsh*t jazz attitude and big mouth were a complete drag, and not at all appreciated by anyone in the control room." Click. I played well enough, but I lost the account because I had to be "Mr. Entertainment" with my big mouth, negating all of the good work I had done up to that point with this client and others in the studio. As embarrassing and shameful as the phone call was, this guy did me a great favor by waking me up to my own baloney, and teaching me a big lesson. When working on a project that's not your own (i.e., most of the time for freelancers), the people in charge have many things on their plate, and the *last* thing anyone needs to worry about is a loud-mouthed musician. Keep your head low, and do good work.

This also applies to asking questions during a rehearsal or recording session. Certainly ask if there's something you need to know in order to do your best work. Much of the time you should be able to figure out the answer yourself without delaying a project or embarrassing a conductor/composer by asking obvious error questions (e.g., pointing out an error on the written part). A little discretion can go a long way in the studio or rehearsal stage. No side talking or joking around. And, for Pete's sake, keep your smartphone away until break time!

Peter: Speaking of smartphones (!)—I was signing autographs after a concert in the beautiful Italian city of Trieste, and at some point I sat myself down when it seemed like I had signed everybody's CD, etc., and became immersed in my phone's mail program, looking for a particular image to share with bassist Benjamin Shepherd. Three men came up to me, two of them supporting their colleague who needed assistance walking (in other words, they came and stood and waited at some discomfort for all involved), and I signaled "moment" while I browsed thoughtlessly on the phone. In other words, the phone/gadget/electronic environment made me completely tone-deaf to these people. After a while when I looked up, they were gone. I failed in the most basic of courtesies, and forever lost that unique opportunity for an exchange of intimacy between strangers.

Speaking of Talking …

Here are some handy suggestions to keep in mind when speaking on mic, making announcements to your audience, etc.

1. Make sure to speak into the mic, and be aware that your voice is supposed to be heard by the audience. Few things are more annoying than someone standing in front of a microphone, speaking, but not actually using it in a way that allows the audience to understand what you're saying.

2. When announcing the musicians' names, introducing them to the audience, *wait* between names during the applause before you speak the next musician's name. Wait until it's quiet; otherwise most or all of the audience will not hear the name you've announced during the applause, etc.

3. No "inside" band jokes on-mic—the audience is not interested and does not care. Period.

4. Don't tell an audience how "beautiful" a piece of music is that you're about to play. They'll hear if it's beautiful or not.

5. When you're finished speaking, make sure that the "talk" or "announce" mic is turned off, either by switching it off yourself (the Shure SM58 with On/Off Switch is the best for this!), or making eye contact with the FOH (front of house) sound person and giving it a light tap to let you know the mic is not "live"— otherwise, there goes your whole mix.

6. And, finally, don't be one of those people that says, "Give it up" over and over while introducing or mentioning a musician's name on-mic. If you do, you'll sound like an idiot.

That band has more mikes than an Irish bar on St. Patrick's Day.—*Jake Hanna* commenting about
The Brecker Brothers Band during their soundcheck in Nice, France

Peter: I generally leave mic choices and placement up to the engineer, whether onstage or in the studio. Depending on the style or sound of the music, I may make a suggestion regarding a specific mic for a particular drum, such as the bass drum. If I'm playing an 18" bass drum tuned up in pitch, I may not want a bass drum mic that brings out or "bumps" the low-end. I will also take note of the placement of a bass drum mic to the resonant head. If it's too close, that may produce what is known as the "proximity effect," which results in an unnatural and exaggerated low-end to the sound (otherwise known as "whoof").

Condenser mics are great but are more prone to feedback onstage than dynamic mics.

Most engineers know all of these things.

Peter: Whenever I'm working with an engineer for the first time, I will shake his or her hand while introducing myself and ask them to let me know if any of my drums are "misbehaving" in the room, etc. This lets them know that it's okay for them to make tuning suggestions, and it creates a sense of trust in the workplace. Both of us may now proceed to work towards getting the best sound as partners rather than a case of musician-against-engineer. Remember, everyone is trying to do the best job possible.

ADVICE: Be nice to your sound person/engineer—he or she controls and determines your mix.

SECTION 5

MAINTAINING A HEALTHY LIFESTYLE (YOU'RE ASKING US?)

PROBLEM: I'm experiencing too much ringing in my ears.

Big problem!

TIP: Exposure to playing your instrument and listening to loud amplified music without ear protection can create a temporary or permanent ringing in the ears, called "tinnitus." Ear protection is the only way to prevent noise-induced hearing loss. Earplugs are small inserts that fit snuggly into the outer ear canal. They are available for purchase in a variety of shapes and sizes, or they can be custom made. We suggest you always carry a pair for protection during soundcheck or to provide silent relief in noisy public places. Do not insert ordinary cotton balls or tissue paper wads into the ear canal, as they are very poor protectors. NOTE: Hearing damage is *not* reversible.

NOTE: If you're in the studio and wearing headphones while the engineer is getting sounds or adjusting knobs, etc., you might want to get into the habit of keeping the phones half-on/half-off your ears, so if there *is* a malfunction where a loud noise is sent out to the headphones, you'll minimize the potential damage to your hearing. We speak from experience on this.

Please consult a medical professional,
and check your hearing at regular intervals.
No pun intended.

Staying Healthy on the Road

Being healthy is not just about what you eat but how you live. Making an effort to eat better and live a healthier life can make a huge difference in your energy, mood, and self-esteem. Here are some tips we recommend to keep you physically and mentally healthy while on the road.

- Don't drive long shifts (switch drivers more frequently). If going it alone, stop every two hours to stretch your legs and rest your eyes.

> If you're traveling by car late at night, stay awake.—*Joe Porcaro*

- Try to get some exercise by either walking, running, stretching, or doing yoga. When staying in hotels, use the pool and/or gym.

- Party in moderation.

- Incorporate relaxation techniques such as deep breathing, focusing on the present, laughing out loud, listening to smooth music, being grateful, visualization, etc.

- Get as much sleep as you can.

- Maintain good relationships.

- Spend time alone by exploring a new city by foot, reading a book, eating at a different restaurant from your travel companions, meditating, etc.

- Distribute the duties amongst all band members.

- Stay hydrated throughout the day by drinking plenty of water.

- Use a hand sanitizer when soap and water aren't available.

- Eat right! Avoid eating too much fast food. Carry a small cooler filled with fresh fruit, dried fruit, trail mix, vegetables, protein bars, etc. Whatever you eat, chew well, and eat with a sense of gratitude. Think positively about the food you're putting into your body.

- Many musicians play their best after they've had some protein.

More Tips for Traveling

Touring is stressful. At some point, someone will have a tantrum about something. Our advice: don't fight it. Give that person space, and allow the rant to pass. And, if and when it seems appropriate, ask the person if you can give them a hug. (In Peter's experience, this works every time.) Here is some additional travel advice.

1. Be courteous, helpful, and nice to others when you travel.

2. Never challenge the authority of anyone wearing a uniform, whether it's a police officer or a doorman.

3. Always approach the knob or handle of a closed door with your fingers curled into a fist (not straightened out). That way, if the door opens suddenly, your fingers will not get injured.

4. No matter where you are in the world, there is no such thing as a private email or text.

5. Get yourself a VPN account for use with hotel (open) internet connections.

6. Bring small bars of soap with you when you travel to Europe; they really come in handy.

7. Same for (in sink) laundry soap.

8. Pack and wear "travel" shirts and travel undergarments.

9. Set your alarm clock or smartphone up across the room so that you need to get out of bed to turn off the alarm. And be sure to check your "AMs" versus "PMs" when setting the alarm!

10. The weather is wacky...pack something warm just in case.

11. Take naps whenever you can. Balance your naps with walks.

Travel Advice from the Pros

Treat everyone kindly—make their day. Drink lots and lots and lots of **water.**
—*John Daversa*

Have respect for others! Smile!
—*Justin DiCioccio*

PLAN FOR EVERY POSSIBLE UNEXPECTED CONTINGENCY.
—*Gary Burton*

Try to enjoy the journey.—*Skip Hadden*

Pack carefully—don't take too much.—*Janet Paulus*

Learn to travel with small bags!—*Rita Marcotulli*

Avoid stress by getting where you need to early.—*Adam Nussbaum*

No expectations. Go with the flow, and when traveling with a group, *don't be late!*—*Matt Harris*

When traveling across time zones, immediately get on the local time. Do whatever it takes to get your body into the rhythm of the new zone, i.e. work out, eat, take vitamins or medications, and sleep.—*Janis Siegel*

Use your free time wisely; make sure you get enough rest.
—*Catina DeLuna*

WHEN YOU ONLY HAVE TIME FOR ONE (warm-up, eat, hang out, or sleep), ALWAYS choose **sleep**!—*Ellen Seeling*

Maintain a network of friends in the various cities/countries you travel to. These familiar faces/resources can help you navigate unfamiliar terrain and help you if you've forgotten to pack a piece of gear!
—*Steve Fidyk*

👍 *Tour Italy whenever possible.*—Alan Pasqua

Never be at the mercy of others for food and water. Always have your own handy.

—Antonio García

Pack as light as you can, and when you get to another time zone—that is now your time zone. Function by the hours there as far as your normal sleep and meals. Really helps in avoiding jet lag. Get to the airport early. An hour early beats a minute late.—Leland Sklar

 Eat and rest well.—Ed Soph

Try to see as much as possible wherever you find yourself.—Tom Ranier

For clothing attire, always start with your socks and work your way up to your jacket.—Don Shelton

Greet the ticket agent with a smile!—Nathan East

👍 **Relax, because things will go haywire.**—Scott Goodman

Take care of yourself on the road. Don't worry about things that are out of your control. Keep aware of all of your travel plans (don't just rely on your tour manager to know everything).—Damian Erskine

Multiple black tee shirts for an all-purpose, fresh "new" look daily.
—Jeff Levenson

Treat others on the road as you would like to be treated, especially if you are the bandleader.—Marc Copland

Eat healthy, drink lots of water, and get as much sleep as possible.—Kenny Aronoff

Be on time on all calls (lobby, soundcheck, etc.), be nice, and stay clean.—Luis Conte

Don't drink too much, and stay in shape.—John Beck

Read up on where you're going so you know what to do and see when you get there.—*Bruce Broughton*

Get out and explore the different places and cultures you visit. Take lots of photos! Learn something!—*John Ramsay*

> *Respect and pay attention to everyone and everything around you—various customs, cultural traits, etc. And* **music!**—*John Clayton*

> **Always praise and thank your stage crew in their handling of your equipment.**—*Bill Platt*

Stay connected to home.—*Ralph Humphrey*

Go out and interact with people, and do your best to learn about their culture.—*Ignacio Berroa*

Get to the airport early.—*David Liebman*

 Be a considerate bandmate.—*Jake Reed*

Always be aware of your environment, and be respectful to all that you meet.—*Gary Hobbs*

> **Eat clean and exercise on the road.**—*Allison Miller*

Always be friendly and respectful. Take walks and experience local sights, sounds, and tastes. Laugh as often as possible.—*Matt Wilson*

Take care of the people that move your instruments.—*Joe Pereira*

What's one night in the eyes of eternity?...To detach some from the quality of hotel rooms.—*Terri Lyne Carrington*

> **Get yourself the best pair of noise-cancelling headphones that you can afford!**—*Danny Seraphine*

Drink lots of water, rest (sleep), and take daily walks.—*Carl Allen*

Get enough sleep.—*Grant Geissman*

Never separate yourself from the group.—*Steve Khan*

When things don't go according to plan, you have to surrender to how it's flowing and figure out how to take pleasure out of whatever is available to you.—Cuong Vu

 Put your suits/clothing in plastic cleaner's bags before putting them in your garment bag or suitcase to minimize wrinkling.—*Jeff Jarvis*

Sleep as much as possible.—*Christian McBride*

Take protein bars wherever you go.—Abbie Conant

Surround yourself with people that share your core values.—*Rick Drumm*

 Always have a pen and notebook handy.—Anne Hills

I always bring canned sardines and rice crackers with me. Where do you eat after a gig at midnight on a Monday night in Fez, Morocco?
—Mike Mainieri

Carry essentials with you in case your bag is lost.—*Danny Gottlieb*

Treat it like a solo: learn when to speak, learn when to joke...learn when to keep silent.—*Otmaro Ruíz*

Make sure your equipment is in tip-top shape, and (in my case) carry extra strings. Being on the road can be lonely so make sure to bring things that keep you occupied: scores to read, your favorite books, etc.—Alyssa Park

While on the road, free meals are wonderful on the budget, but overeating is the worst, just because the meals are on the artist.—*Hal Blaine*

Seek out the healthiest food choices you can. Bring a good pillow. (I travel with two!)—*Will Lee*

I try to maintain some structure when I am on the road. Try to get enough rest and get used to exercising, even if it's running in place or stretching in your hotel room. Save your energy for the bandstand—that's why you are there! (Although the post-gig hangs can be pretty fun sometimes!) But, strive for balance in your music and in your life, which means maybe you don't hang hard every single night.

—*Gordon Goodwin*

Pack only what you need. Be patient, flexible, and understanding. Anything can happen, and if you do enough traveling, it will.—*Tim Ishii*

Be sure to experience your surroundings beyond the performance.—*Gary Motley*

Noise-cancelling headphones and tons of water on the plane, plus a high-quality neck pillow to avoid pinching cervical nerves and muscles if you doze off.—*William Kanengiser*

Always go to the gig the day *before* your concert if possible. With the "hub system," compared to travel in the '70s and '80s, there are so many ways that your flight can be delayed or cancelled by some nationwide "domino effect."
—*Chris Brubeck*

Hope for the best, expect the worst. Traveling to perform these days is difficult because every entity presuming to provide all the different elements of travel to the customer does so in the cheapest manner possible. Travel is no longer about the customer, but rather about making the most money for the provider—the customer be damned. Some of us older musicians remember when travel was the opposite, actually a real pleasure.—*Marvin Stamm*

Take the first flight out.—*Bill Cunliffe*

Be on time and get enough rest.—*Chuck Berghofer*

Music, music, music, books, books, books. Podcasts, too. Interact with your environment, see the sights, and take advantage of opportunities, experiences, and adventures. Take care of yourself.—*Fred Simon*

Be open to seeing new places in the world, but do some research. Don't do things that could compromise your safety, and learn some key phrases in the languages of the places you are going.—John L. Worley, Jr.

Be especially courteous to *all* airport security staff!—*Neil Percy*

Travel light. You'd be amazed how little you need!—*Christine Pendrill*

Sleep when you can. Don't get angry with anything because it just might be fate.—Makoto Ozone

Embrace the local time zone.—*John Goldsby*

I have **traveled** far and wide and have **learnt a lot** from the everyday **life** of **local people**, as well as the natural **features** and climate of **each** place. The things **I have gained** by getting **right into the lives** of the **local** people, rather than by **seeing them** from the outside through glass windows, have become the **food for my music.**—*Sadao Watanabe*

THE BUSINESS OF MUSIC

The Art of Networking

If you don't know how to network within the music industry or feel uncomfortable networking, here are a few tips to help you navigate and build a strong network within the industry.

1. Networking begins with both intention and initiative.

2. True business relationships take time to build and nurture. They also hinge on credibility.

3. Start with your peers and/or your local music scene.

4. If you want to meet artists, promoters, labels, agents, manufacturers, and managers, you have to be active. Attend music-industry networking events, join industry organizations, and attend jam sessions, showcases, and songwriter nights.

5. Try being the type of person people would like to know more rather than someone they can use or who wants to use them.

6. Don't be fake! People will tend to remember those that are sincere, helpful, charming, or funny as opposed to those who had the best sales pitch or said they had an amazing demo to share. Make sure you ask about them, why they are there, etc. Small gestures of kindness will go a long way.

7. Don't take everything personally. Learning to deal with rejection is part of the process and something that all musicians experience.

8. Don't burn bridges. Just because someone may not like you or what you do, holding a grudge or thinking about vendettas is a waste of time and energy, and is counterproductive.

9. The best industry relationships are those that are mutually beneficial for both parties. Don't expect a friend or someone in a position of power to constantly do favors for you without you giving something back in return.

10. No matter what field you're in, remember that people want to help those they like. Charisma and charm help, but taking the time to really engage with someone is going to yield the best results. Developing relationships and good social habits takes effort and time.

11. Limit the time you take with someone. Although you want to make a good impression, remember that they are there for a specific reason as well, and that it's important to let them get back to what they were doing.

12. Don't start the conversation with a list of your accomplishments. Instead, begin with a genuine topic and clear communication.

13. Body language is very important. Receptive body language includes moving or leaning closer to the person you're talking to; relaxed, uncrossed legs; good eye contact; a genuine smile; and engaging in the conversation. Non-receptive body language includes moving or moving away from the person; crossed arms or legs; looking away or around for someone else.

14. Whenever you meet someone new, make sure you follow up with at least a "thank you" email or letter. If someone refers you to someone else, make sure you thank him or her for doing so as well.

15. Don't be afraid to ask for specific referrals.

16. Always carry business cards with you, and save the business cards and contact information you receive from others.

17. Keep your promises. If you told someone you would make a call or do something specific, make sure you follow through.

18. Don't be pushy or annoying! And, whatever you do, do NOT scrunch the person's hand you're shaking *or* attempt to pivot from a normal handshake into some angled-1970s-hip-hand-shake that risks pulling the unwary recipient's hand into a vulnerable position that pulls the thumb in a way it was not designed to take. You not only run the risk of impairing the recipient's ability to play his or her instrument, but the person you do that to will never forgive you—and be right.

Should I Join Music Organizations?

There are many organizations available to help support both the creativity and well-being of the music community at large. Here are a few of the organizations you should consider joining and/or reaching out to for help and/or advice:

American Federation of Musicians (AFM)

American Society of Composers, Authors and Publishers (ASCAP)

Broadcast Music, Inc. (BMI)

Church Music Publishers Association (CMPA)

Country Music Association (CMA)

Jazz Education Network (JEN)

The Latin Academy of Recording Arts & Sciences, Inc.

Music Business Association (Music Biz)

Music Managers Forum (MMF-US)

NAMM (National Association of Music Merchants)

National Music Publishers' Association (NMPA)

The Recording Academy

SESAC

Songwriters Guild of America (SGA)

The Society of Composers and Lyricists (SCL)

American Society of Music Arrangers and Composers (ASMAC)

Should I Attend Music Conventions?

Yes! Conventions, such as the Jazz Education Network (JEN), The Midwest Clinic: International Band and Orchestra Conference, and NAMM are excellent opportunities to not only see the latest and greatest instruments and gear, but to attend master classes, clinics, and concerts, and to network with other musicians and industry companies/leaders.

How Can Social Media Best Be Utilized?

Don't spend your life there. Maintain a healthy balance, and keep your social media posts short, entertaining, informative, and fun. Too much is a turn-off, so keep it short and sweet. A clever campaign of info combined with good sounds is always of interest to music lovers.

Try not to be tone-deaf when posting. The operative word here is **timing**. Be sensitive to world events (especially regarding the fate of others in the news).

If you're on Facebook, **band pages** are more effective than personal pages. Post your cat and dog videos on your personal page, and not on your band page. Twitter is useful. Instagram is fun, but only if you post stuff that sounds or looks cool. Obviously, YouTube works well for video.

Speaking from experience: if you're equipment is lost or stolen, social media is a great way to solicit help from the world-at-large. Given the chance, more people will prove helpful rather than hurtful online.

Get yourself a website, and don't believe everything you read on the internet.

How Much Self-Promotion Is Too Much?

Here is where **the other** comes into play. Too many "I," "me," and "my" references are, frankly, boring. We shine the best light on ourselves when we praise others. Your music will speak loudest and best for you. With that being said, it's okay to let people know what you're doing, and it's okay to be proud of your accomplishments. But it's just like anything else in life. If you need to keep reminding people how good you are, then your music is not doing the job, and you'd be wise to get back into the practice room.

Music speaks louder than words.

Negotiation

Whether you're considering a written offer or having a verbal discussion, the devil can be in the details when it comes to negotiating a deal. For any written contract, you should seek qualified legal counsel and representation.

If you're being asked to do a gig by, say, telephone or email, here's how to handle such discussions. First, always thank the musician or artist rep for the interest in having you join a particular project. Once you check the calendar and confirm your availability, ask to listen to some of the project so you can confidently determine if you're the "right" musician for that project (this approach is more polite than saying, "I want to see if your music sucks or not before I say yes..."), unless you know the artist's work. Then, it's a matter of agreeing on the terms.

Fee

Will you receive gross or net (after taxes) pay if the project is a foreign engagement?

Does your fee represent a "favored-nations" status (i.e., your offer is no lower than anyone else's)?

Manner and timing of payment? (Advance? Direct deposit? Check? Cash? Union or non-union?)

Travel expenses and conditions (economy or business class)?

Per Diem (a daily allowance for food and typical road expenses)?

Recording

How many hours/how many songs?

Audio/visual rights (video)?

Do I get album credit?

Can I thank or mention the companies of the products I endorse on the album?

If I'm with another record label, do I need to get permission to appear on this album/label? (It depends on your contract with that other label—seek professional legal counsel.)

Be polite. Be prepared to say no if you don't like the offer. If someone really wants you, he or she will improve the offer—but you need to know that you're okay if you're not pursued.

Other than that, we recommend you join the American Federation of Musicians and record as a union member!

Don't Be Afraid to Say No

Peter: My wife was on the phone once with a contractor about a recording project—an album I was not particularly keen on doing—so I slipped her a note suggesting she ask for "triple scale." The contractor reacted with horror and dismay, informing her, "That's more than we pay so and so," to which she replied, "I understand...um, would you like so and so's phone number? I have it right here..." The guy agreed to our fee request. Know your worth.

Otherwise, be humble and do the work, because it's always good to do the work. Experience is priceless!

With that being said, my professor at Indiana University (George Gaber) often counseled me on the **importance of being able to say no**. If a gig conflicts with an important family plan, say no to the gig, and prioritize your family. If someone wants you, he or she will always call you again.

Maynard Ferguson's Rule on Charity

Peter: Trumpeter/bandleader Maynard Ferguson once told me, "If you finish a gig and the club owner or concert promoter cries the money blues to you, don't accept less than what was originally agreed upon. However, once you are paid in full, *then* you can return some of the cash back to the promoter or owner, and your generosity will be better remembered and appreciated."

To be honest, I've never tried this.

Burn Out

You'll often hear pedagogues, guest speakers, or music do-gooders say something along the lines of, "Every time I touch my instrument, I want to make beautiful music ..." or, "Every time I go to deliver a performance, I am excited by it ..." This is basically feel-good/Hallmark greeting card advice. It is okay sometimes to not want to play your instrument. That's natural. It is also normal to have a love-hate relationship with your instrument. It's up to each of us to figure out how to stabilize our confidence and professionalism while reconciling our doubts, fears, or resentments. Here's some Peter advice for you:

Life is short. Have fun.

Endorsements and Music Industry Companies

QUESTION: How do I get an endorsement deal with an instrument company?

ANSWER: By not asking for one!

This may seem counterintuitive, but the best way to receive something is to neither expect it nor ask for it. Certainly make yourself and your interest known, but the latter is best expressed by simply conveying your admiration for a brand. That may include a long history of using a particular product (or products) made by a company. A recommendation made by a currently endorsed artist doesn't hurt.

Unsolicited contacts and pitches made by musicians to companies usually end up in the trash, especially if they're expecting free gear out of the gate. By the way, most of the gear is not "free" in the sense that it's given to you and you own it. Technically, the equipment belongs to the manufacturer or music company distributing a company's products. With perishables like drumsticks, drumheads, mouth pieces, and reeds this becomes a moot point, but the instruments we play? These belong to those companies; otherwise you may be liable to pay taxes on the goods.

Let your music do the talking. "Talent will out," as the saying goes. Once a company becomes aware of you, what you can do, and the type of person you are, they will come to you. An obvious bit of advice: Don't act like a jerk.

General Business Etiquette and Strategies

Don't be a jerk. Oh! We already said that.

Behavior on and off the bandstand is less of a strategy and more of a way of life, to be honest. Don't be "nice" to someone because it might improve your chances of getting something. Be "nice" because you like to be pleasant to people and to leave a room with more smiles rather than less. So, it's always good to be polite.

Here's an important concept to remember from the worlds of technology and business, known as "the failure of the last mile." Essentially, you do not want the end result of your hard work on a project to be remembered only for an unfortunate final word or impression that undoes all of the good will you've been building up by means of being polite, engaged, playing well, and so on. We've been guilty, or have fallen prey, to this on numerous occasions, and it's almost always avoidable. Take a deep breath, and think before you speak.

Be grateful for the opportunity, *any* opportunity to make music, and don't say anything stupid on your way out the door.

Otherwise, make certain that there are no misunderstandings on when and how you are to be paid for your work, and for what that work entails. Be a man or woman of your word. And make sure you get it in writing.

Music Copyrights

Dave: As a person who has worked in the music publishing industry for years, I have put together some questions/answers below regarding basic music copyright law. These are only intended as a starting point for quick reference. Because technology and copyright laws are always evolving, we suggest you consult with an attorney or contact the United States Copyright Office at *copyright.gov* when dealing with questions and/or issues outside the scope of this book.

1. What is a copyright?

A legal and exclusive right granted to an author, composer, or publisher to publish and sell literary, musical, dramatic, or artistic creations.

2. Do copyright laws vary from country to country?

Yes

3. Do I have to file for a copyright each time I write a new composition?

Not necessarily, as the current copyright law states that a work is automatically copyrighted the moment it is affixed in a tangible medium (e.g., on paper or on an audio recording). However, by registering your work, you establish a public record of your copyright, and you are provided additional protections if a dispute or infringement occurs.

4. Does a piece of music need to include a copyright notice?

Though we recommended doing so, it is not necessary in order to have the work protected. The copyright notice is optional for unpublished works, foreign works, or works published on or after March 1, 1989. However, by including the symbol and notice, you can prevent a defendant in an infringement case from using an innocent infringement defense to limit their liability for damages or injunctive relief.

5. What is meant by "public domain"?

The term public domain refers to music that belongs to the public and therefore can be used by anyone. An arrangement of a public domain song, however, can be copyrighted if it was created in 1923 or later.

6. How long does a copyright last?

Current U.S. copyright law extends protection for the life of the author, or last surviving author, plus 70 years. This is based on the U.S. Copyright Act of 1976 that took effect on January 1, 1978. Remember, copyright laws will vary from country to country.

7. Is music that is out of print considered public domain?

Not necessarily.

8. Can I copy music in an educational or non-profit setting?

Not necessarily.

9. Can I scan printed music without obtaining permission?

Legally, no.

10. Can I post or share copyrighted recordings (MP3, WAV, etc.)?

Legally, no.

11. Can an idea for a song or composition be copyrighted?

Unless realized in a tangible form, a copyright cannot protect an idea or concept.

12. Can I copyright the name of my performing group/ensemble?

No, as copyright law does not protect names.

13. Are titles copyrightable?

Legally, no.

14. Are chords copyrightable?

Legally, no.

15. Can I earn money if my song or composition is played?

Yes, but you'll need to join a performing rights organization (ASCAP, BMI, SESAC, etc.) first.

16. What's a performing rights organization?

An organization that monitors the public performance of music, represents license venues, collects play lists and license fees, and distributes royalties to the copyright holders, composers, and authors.

17. Can I copyright multiple tunes for a single fee?

Yes, if the tunes are submitted as a collection with a collective title. If there are multiple writers within the collection, at least one writer needs to be common throughout.

18. What does the symbol ℗ mean?

This is a copyright symbol used for tangible sound recordings such as CDs and vinyl recordings. It usually appears at the bottom of the label art.

19. What does the symbol © mean?

This is a copyright notice symbol usually found at the bottom of the first page of music. The symbol, or the word "copyright," is usually followed by the year and the name of the rights holder.

20. If my permission request is denied from the publisher, is there an alternative option I can pursue?

No, as the copyright owner/administrator has the right to grant or deny any requests.

21. What is a mechanical license?

A license that grants the rights to record, reproduce, and distribute copyrighted musical compositions (songs) through CDs, permanent digital downloads, interactive streams, and all other audio distribution formats. This license is compulsory, and the rates are set by Congress. Musicians can register their original works or arrangements of public domain compositions through The Harry Fox Agency, who will license, collect, and distribute royalties on behalf of the musical copyright owner(s).

22. What is a synchronization license?

A license used for allowing the creation of videos with music (whether or not they are sold). Composers/writers can sign with a publisher or third-party submission company who will seek out placement and royalty collection for synchronization licenses by utilizing their pre-existing relationships with music supervisors and studios/production companies. One can also write/sell/license their music to libraries who market music catalogs and offer blanket licenses for compositions and recordings based on a high-volume business, with rates set based on medium, type of program, broadcast day and time, etc.

23. **Where can I obtain copyright forms, and how much does it cost to register a work?**

Please visit the U.S. Copyright Office website at *copyright.gov*. For additional questions regarding performance rights, and mechanical and synchronization licenses, please visit the Harry Fox Agency at *https://www.harryfox.com/find_out/faq.php*, ASCAP at *https://www.ascap.com/help/ascap-licensing*, and BMI at *https://www.bmi.com/licensing/entry/types_of_copyrights*.

COPYRIGHT FORM TX

 Form TX

Detach and read these instructions before completing this form.
Make sure all applicable spaces have been filled in before you return this form.

▬▬▬▬▬▬▬▬▬▬ BASIC INFORMATION ▬▬▬▬▬▬▬▬▬▬

When to Use This Form: Use Form TX for registration of published or unpublished nondramatic literary works, excluding periodicals or serial issues. This class includes a wide variety of works: fiction, nonfiction, poetry, textbooks, reference works, directories, catalogs, advertising copy, compilations of information, and computer programs. For periodicals and serials, use Form SE.

Unpublished works: This form may be used to register one unpublished work. This form cannot be used to register a "collection" of two or more unpublished works. Any paper application submitted with more than one unpublished work may be refused. To register multiple unpublished works, you must use the online application for "A Group of Unpublished Works." For information about the online application, see *Multiple Works* (Circular 34).

Deposit to Accompany Application: An application for copyright registration must be accompanied by a deposit consisting of copies or phonorecords representing the entire work for which registration is to be made. The following are the general deposit requirements as set forth in the statute:
Unpublished Work: Deposit one complete copy (or phonorecord)
Published Work: Deposit two complete copies (or one phonorecord) of the best edition.
Work First Published Outside the United States: Deposit one complete copy (or phonorecord) of the first foreign edition.
Contribution to a Collective Work: Deposit one complete copy (or phonorecord) of the best edition of the collective work.

The Copyright Notice: Before March 1, 1989, the use of copyright notice was mandatory on all published works, and any work first published before that date should have carried a notice. For works first published on and after March 1, 1989, use of the copyright notice is optional. For more information about copyright notice, see *Copyright Notice* (Circular 3).

For Further Information: To speak to a Copyright Office staff member, call (202) 707-3000 or 1-877-476-0778 (toll free). Recorded information is available 24 hours a day. Order forms and other publications from the address in space 9 or call the Forms and Publications Hotline at (202) 707-9100. Access and download circulars, certain forms, and other information from the Copyright Office website at *www.copyright.gov.*

▬▬▬▬▬▬▬▬▬▬ LINE-BY-LINE INSTRUCTIONS ▬▬▬▬▬▬▬▬▬▬

Please type or print using black ink. The form is used to produce the certificate.

1 SPACE 1: Title

Title of This Work: Every work submitted for copyright registration must be given a title to identify that particular work. If the copies or phonorecords of the work bear a title or an identifying phrase that could serve as a title, transcribe that wording *completely* and *exactly* on the application. Indexing of the registration and future identification of the work will depend on the information you give here.

Previous or Alternative Titles: Complete this space if there are any additional titles for the work under which someone searching for the registration might be likely to look or under which a document pertaining to the work might be recorded.

Publication as a Contribution: If the work being registered is a contribution to a periodical, serial, or collection, give the title of the contribution in the "Title of This Work" space. Then, in the line headed "Publication as a Contribution," give information about the collective work in which the contribution appeared.

2 SPACE 2: Author(s)

General Instructions: After reading these instructions, decide who are the "authors" of this work for copyright purposes. Then, unless the work is a "collective work," give the requested information about every "author" who contributed any appreciable amount of copyrightable matter to this version of the work. If you need further space, request Continuation Sheets. In the case of a collective work, such as an anthology, collection of essays, or encyclopedia, give information about the author of the collective work as a whole.

Name of Author: The fullest form of the author's name should be given. Unless the work was "made for hire," the individual who actually created the work is its "author." In the case of a work made for hire, the statute provides that "the employer or other person for whom the work was prepared is considered the author."

What Is a "Work Made for Hire"? A "work made for hire" is defined as (1) "a work prepared by an employee within the scope of his or her employment"; or (2) "a work specially ordered or commissioned for use as a contribution to a collective work, as a part of a motion picture or other audiovisual work, as a translation, as a supplementary work, as a compilation, as an instructional text, as a test, as answer material for a test, or as an atlas, if the parties expressly agree in a written instrument signed by them that the works shall be considered a work made for hire." If you have checked "Yes" to indicate that the work was "made for hire," you must give the full legal name of the employer (or other person for whom the work was prepared). You may also include the name of the employee along with the name of the employer (for example: "Elster Publishing Co., employer for hire of John Ferguson").

"Anonymous" or "Pseudonymous" Work: An author's contribution to a work is "anonymous" if that author is not identified on the copies or phonorecords of the work. An author's contribution to a work is "pseudonymous" if that author is identified on the copies or phonorecords under a fictitious name. If the work is "anonymous" you may: (1) leave the line blank; or (2) state "anonymous" on the line; or (3) reveal the author's identity. If the work is "pseudonymous" you may: (1) leave the line blank; or (2) give the pseudonym and identify it as such (for example: "Huntley Haverstock, pseudonym"); or (3) reveal the author's name, making clear which is the real name and which is the pseudonym (for example, "Judith Barton, whose pseudonym is Madeline Elster"). However, the citizenship or domicile of the author *must* be given in all cases.

Dates of Birth and Death: If the author is dead, the statute requires that the year of death be included in the application unless the work is anonymous or pseudonymous. The author's birth date is optional but is useful as a form of identification. Leave this space blank if the author's contribution was a "work made for hire."

Author's Nationality or Domicile: Give the country of which the author is a citizen or the country in which the author is domiciled. Nationality or domicile *must* be given in all cases.

Nature of Authorship: After the words "Nature of Authorship," give a brief general statement of the nature of this particular author's contribution to the work. Examples: "Entire text"; "Coauthor of entire text"; "Computer program"; "Editorial revisions"; "Compilation and English translation"; "New text."

SPACE 3: Creation and Publication

General Instructions: Do not confuse "creation" with "publication." Every application for copyright registration must state "the year in which creation of the work was completed." Give the date and nation of first publication only if the work has been published.

Creation: Under the statute, a work is "created" when it is fixed in a copy or phonorecord for the first time. Where a work has been prepared over a period of time, the part of the work existing in fixed form on a particular date constitutes the created work on that date. The date you give here should be the year in which the author completed the particular version for which registration is now being sought, even if other versions exist or if further changes or additions are planned.

Publication: The statute defines "publication" as "the distribution of copies or phonorecords of a work to the public by sale or other transfer of ownership, or by rental, lease, or lending." A work is also "published" if there has been an "offering to distribute copies or phonorecords to a group of persons for purposes of further distribution, public performance, or public display." Give the full date (month, day, year) when, and the country where, publication first occurred. If first publication took place simultaneously in the United States and other countries, it is sufficient to state "U.S.A."

SPACE 4: Claimant(s)

Name(s) and Address(es) of Copyright Claimant(s): Give the name(s) and address(es) of the copyright claimant(s) in this work even if the claimant is the same as the author. Copyright in a work belongs initially to the author of the work (including, in the case of a work made for hire, the employer or other person for whom the work was prepared). The copyright claimant is either the author of the work or a person or organization to whom the copyright initially belonging to the author has been transferred.

Transfer: The statute provides that, if the copyright claimant is not the author, the application for registration must contain "a brief statement of how the claimant obtained ownership of the copyright." If any copyright claimant named in space 4 is not an author named in space 2, give a brief statement explaining how the claimant(s) obtained ownership of the copyright. Examples: "By written contract"; "Transfer of all rights by author"; "Assignment"; "By will." Do not attach transfer documents or other attachments or riders.

SPACE 5: Previous Registration

General Instructions: The questions in space 5 are intended to show whether an earlier registration has been made for this work and, if so, whether there is any basis for a new registration. As a general rule, only one basic copyright registration can be made for the same version of a particular work.

Same Version: If this version is substantially the same as the work covered by a previous registration, a second registration is not generally possible unless: (1) the work has been registered in unpublished form and a second registration is now being sought to cover this first published edition; or (2)

someone other than the author is identified as copyright claimant in the earlier registration, and the author is now seeking registration in his or her own name. If either of these two exceptions applies, check the appropriate box and give the earlier registration number and date. Otherwise, do not submit Form TX. Instead, write the Copyright Office for information about supplementary registration or recordation of transfers of copyright ownership.

Changed Version: If the work has been changed and you are now seeking registration to cover the additions or revisions, check the last box in space 5, give the earlier registration number and date, and complete both parts of space 6 in accordance with the instructions below.

Previous Registration Number and Date: If more than one previous registration has been made for the work, give the number and date of the latest registration.

SPACE 6: Derivative Work or Compilation

General Instructions: Complete space 6 if this work is a "changed version," "compilation," or "derivative work" and if it incorporates one or more earlier works that have already been published or registered for copyright or that have fallen into the public domain. A "compilation" is defined as "a work formed by the collection and assembling of preexisting materials or of data that are selected, coordinated, or arranged in such a way that the resulting work as a whole constitutes an original work of authorship." A "derivative work" is "a work based on one or more preexisting works." Examples of derivative works include translations, fictionalizations, abridgments, condensations, or "any other form in which a work may be recast, transformed, or adapted." Derivative works also include works "consisting of editorial revisions, annotations, or other modifications" if these changes, as a whole, represent an original work of authorship.

Preexisting Material (space 6a): For derivative works, complete this space *and* space 6b. In space 6a identify the preexisting work that has been recast, transformed, or adapted. The preexisting work may be material that has been previously published, previously registered, or that is in the public domain. An example of preexisting material might be: "Russian version of Goncharov's 'Oblomov.'"

Material Added to This Work (space 6b): Give a brief, general statement of the new material covered by the copyright claim for which registration is sought. *Derivative work* examples include: "Foreword, editing, critical annotations"; "Translation"; "Chapters 11–17." If the work is a *compilation*, describe both the compilation itself and the material that has been compiled. Example: "Compilation of certain 1917 speeches by Woodrow Wilson." A work may be both a derivative work and compilation, in which case a sample statement might be: "Compilation and additional new material."

SPACE 7,8,9: Fee, Correspondence, Certification, Return Address

Deposit Account: If you maintain a Deposit Account in the Copyright Office, identify it in space 7a. Otherwise leave the space blank and send the fee with your application and deposit.

Correspondence (space 7b): Give the name, address, area code, telephone number, fax number, and email address (if available) of the person to be consulted if correspondence about this application becomes necessary.

Certification (space 8): The application cannot be accepted unless it bears the date and the *handwritten signature* of the author or other copyright claimant, or of the owner of exclusive right(s), or of the duly authorized agent of author, claimant, or owner of exclusive right(s).

Address for Return of Certificate (space 9): The address box must be completed legibly because the certificate will be returned in a window envelope.

COPYRIGHT FORM TX, cont.

Copyright Office fees are subject to change. For current fees, check the Copyright Office website at *www.copyright.gov*, write the Copyright Office, or call (202) 707-3000.

Clear Form

Form TX
For a Nondramatic Literary Work
UNITED STATES COPYRIGHT OFFICE

REGISTRATION NUMBER

Privacy Act Notice: Sections 408-410 of title 17 of the *United States Code* authorize the Copyright Office to collect the personally identifying information requested on this form in order to process the application for copyright registration. By providing this information you are agreeing to routine uses of the information that include publication to give legal notice of your copyright claim as required by 17 U.S.C. §705. It will appear in the Office's online catalog. If you do not provide the information requested, registration may be refused or delayed, and you may not be entitled to certain relief, remedies, and benefits under the copyright law.

TX   TXU
EFFECTIVE DATE OF REGISTRATION

Month   Day   Year

DO NOT WRITE ABOVE THIS LINE. IF YOU NEED MORE SPACE, USE A SEPARATE CONTINUATION SHEET.

1

TITLE OF THIS WORK ▼

PREVIOUS OR ALTERNATIVE TITLES ▼

PUBLICATION AS A CONTRIBUTION If this work was published as a contribution to a periodical, serial, or collection, give information about the collective work in which the contribution appeared.   **Title of Collective Work ▼**

If published in a periodical or serial give: Volume ▼   Number ▼   Issue Date ▼   On Pages ▼

2 a

NAME OF AUTHOR ▼

DATES OF BIRTH AND DEATH
Year Born ▼   Year Died ▼

Was this contribution to the work a "work made for hire"?
☐ Yes
☐ No

AUTHOR'S NATIONALITY OR DOMICILE
Name of Country
OR { Citizen of _____
      Domiciled in _____

WAS THIS AUTHOR'S CONTRIBUTION TO THE WORK
Anonymous?   ☐ Yes ☐ No
Pseudonymous? ☐ Yes ☐ No
If the answer to either of these questions is "Yes," see detailed instructions.

NATURE OF AUTHORSHIP Briefly describe nature of material created by this author in which copyright is claimed. ▼

NOTE
Under the law, the "author" of a "work made for hire" is generally the employer, not the employee (see instructions). For any part of this work that was "made for hire" check "Yes" in the space provided, give the employer (or other person for whom the work was prepared) as "Author" of that part, and leave the space for dates of birth and death blank.

b

NAME OF AUTHOR ▼

DATES OF BIRTH AND DEATH
Year Born ▼   Year Died ▼

Was this contribution to the work a "work made for hire"?
☐ Yes
☐ No

AUTHOR'S NATIONALITY OR DOMICILE
Name of Country
OR { Citizen of _____
      Domiciled in _____

WAS THIS AUTHOR'S CONTRIBUTION TO THE WORK
Anonymous?   ☐ Yes ☐ No
Pseudonymous? ☐ Yes ☐ No
If the answer to either of these questions is "Yes," see detailed instructions.

NATURE OF AUTHORSHIP Briefly describe nature of material created by this author in which copyright is claimed. ▼

c

NAME OF AUTHOR ▼

DATES OF BIRTH AND DEATH
Year Born ▼   Year Died ▼

Was this contribution to the work a "work made for hire"?
☐ Yes
☐ No

AUTHOR'S NATIONALITY OR DOMICILE
Name of Country
OR { Citizen of _____
      Domiciled in _____

WAS THIS AUTHOR'S CONTRIBUTION TO THE WORK
Anonymous?   ☐ Yes ☐ No
Pseudonymous? ☐ Yes ☐ No
If the answer to either of these questions is "Yes," see detailed instructions.

NATURE OF AUTHORSHIP Briefly describe nature of material created by this author in which copyright is claimed. ▼

3 a

YEAR IN WHICH CREATION OF THIS WORK WAS COMPLETED   This information must be given in all cases.
Year

b DATE AND NATION OF FIRST PUBLICATION OF THIS PARTICULAR WORK
Complete this information ONLY if this work has been published.
Month _____ Day _____ Year _____
Nation

4

See instructions before completing this space.

COPYRIGHT CLAIMANT(S) Name and address must be given even if the claimant is the same as the author given in space 2. ▼

TRANSFER If the claimant(s) named here in space 4 is (are) different from the author(s) named in space 2, give a brief statement of how the claimant(s) obtained ownership of the copyright. ▼

APPLICATION RECEIVED

ONE DEPOSIT RECEIVED

TWO DEPOSITS RECEIVED

FUNDS RECEIVED

DO NOT WRITE HERE
OFFICE USE ONLY

MORE ON BACK ▶
· Complete all applicable spaces (numbers 5-9) on the reverse side of this page.
· See detailed instructions.   · Sign the form at line 8.

DO NOT WRITE HERE
Page 1 of _____ pages

COPYRIGHT FORM TX, cont.

EXAMINED BY	FORM TX
CHECKED BY	
CORRESPONDENCE ☐ Yes	FOR COPYRIGHT OFFICE USE ONLY

DO NOT WRITE ABOVE THIS LINE. IF YOU NEED MORE SPACE, USE A SEPARATE CONTINUATION SHEET.

PREVIOUS REGISTRATION Has registration for this work, or for an earlier version of this work, already been made in the Copyright Office?

☐ Yes ☐ No If your answer is "Yes," why is another registration being sought? (Check appropriate box.) ▼

a. ☐ This is the first published edition of a work previously registered in unpublished form.

b. ☐ This is the first application submitted by this author as copyright claimant.

c. ☐ This is a changed version of the work, as shown by space 6 on this application.

If your answer is "Yes," give: **Previous Registration Number** ▶   **Year of Registration** ▶

5

DERIVATIVE WORK OR COMPILATION

Preexisting Material Identify any preexisting work or works that this work is based on or incorporates. ▼

6 a

See instructions before completing this space.

Material Added to This Work Give a brief, general statement of the material that has been added to this work and in which copyright is claimed. ▼

b

DEPOSIT ACCOUNT If the registration fee is to be charged to a deposit account established in the Copyright Office, give name and number of account.

Name ▼   **Account Number** ▼

7 a

CORRESPONDENCE Give name and address to which correspondence about this application should be sent. Name/Address/Apt/City/State/Zip ▼

b

Area code and daytime telephone number ▶   Fax number ▶

Email ▶

CERTIFICATION* I, the undersigned, hereby certify that I am the

Check only one ▶
☐ author
☐ other copyright claimant
☐ owner of exclusive right(s)
☐ authorized agent of _____

of the work identified in this application and that the statements made by me in this application are correct to the best of my knowledge.

Name of author or other copyright claimant, or owner of exclusive right(s) ▲

8

Typed or printed name and date ▼ If this application gives a date of publication in space 3, do not sign and submit it before that date.

_____ Date ▶ _____

Handwritten signature ▼

9

Certificate will be mailed in window envelope to this address:

Name ▼

Number/Street/Apt ▼

City/State/Zip ▼

YOU MUST:
· Complete all necessary spaces
· Sign your application in space 8

SEND ALL 3 ELEMENTS IN THE SAME PACKAGE:
1. Application form
2. Nonrefundable filing fee in check or money order payable to Register of Copyrights
3. Deposit material

MAIL TO:
Library of Congress
Copyright Office-TX
101 Independence Avenue SE
Washington, DC 20559

*17 U.S.C. §506(e): Any person who knowingly makes a false representation of a material fact in the application for copyright registration provided for by section 409, or in any written statement filed in connection with the application, shall be fined not more than $2,500.

Form TX–Full Reviewed: 03/2019 Printed on recycled paper

Business Advice from the Pros

PRACTICE THE BUSINESS SIDE OF YOUR CAREER AS MUCH AS YOU DO THE MUSICAL SIDE.
—George S. Clinton

Always ask the hard questions up front (don't avoid the money talk—people so often leave it out of the conversation!), and learn to do so in a way that communicates respect and integrity, with kindness, firmness, and calm.
—Jennifer Barnes

Get it in writing! If you're booking your own group, make sure you have a contract or an email detailing the terms. And, get a deposit. If the purchaser won't agree to these, run away! They're not serious anyway.
—Ellen Seeling

Don't work for free.—Bruce Broughton

Live simply, keep your expenses low, and save for a rainy day.—John Riley

Don't blow your money living beyond your means to impress. Get sound investment advice early.—Vinnie Colaiuta

Keep good records so you can make good records.
—Charlie Bisharat

Remember to factor in preparation, rehearsal, and travel time when deciding whether a gig is worth it. Chances are that most opportunities that come your way will either **A** be with great **people**, **B** **pay** well, or **C** be **prestigious**. In my experience, it's always been best for me to try to get at least two of those things, if not all three (if possible) for any work I accept. This was not always the case when I was young and just trying to gain experience—but has definitely worked for me as a professional with a family.
—Glenn Kotche

> *Be flexible but always make sure you get what you need to be comfortable and perform well (space, lighting, pay, etc.). If you can't get what you need, don't be afraid to say no.—Janet Paulus*

Be the very best you can be, and *always* be professional. *Never* complain... there's always someone lurking around who can do it at least as well as you...often better!—*Jiggs Whigham*

Find a partner who's good at what you're not.—*Brian Malouf*

Get to know as many details as possible about a gig you are invited to play before saying yes.
—*Catina DeLuna*

Thank the people who employ you: by being grateful, by contributing to a good vibe on the gig, by assisting with equipment, by having substitute players ready when needed. Getting work means much more than playing well.
—*Antonio García*

Give business details as much love and attention as you give your music.
—*John Daversa*

Never underestimate the importance of the business aspect. Study. Learn.—*Dan Carlin*

When someone contacts you, get back to them as soon as possible, even if just to acknowledge that you heard from them. Then answer all business-related emails, texts, and voice messages as quickly as possible, and don't be ashamed, embarrassed, or intimidated to ask for the money, the terms and details of the event, your personal billing, travel conditions, etc., that you believe you're entitled to. Last, but not least, always remember to write a "Thank You!" note to people.
—*Paul Wertico*

Embrace social media, and be in control of your brand. Ultimately no one will sell "you" better than you. You can promote yourself without looking like a "self-promoter." And unless you're an established leader or sideman, be flexible and willing to work for less money if you feel there's potential for it to lead to bigger things. Build your résumé.
—*John DeChristopher*

Diversify your income streams, and don't blow it all when the work is coming in. There are always dry times ahead.—Damian Erskine

Be imaginative and clear with your intentions. Take care of your bandmates and, if you are a leader, your bandmembers.
—*Matt Wilson*

Make everyone you meet *want* to work with you. The competition is enormous. Likability often wins the day. Be flexible and open to suggestions from producers and artists. In the end, they *must* be satisfied.—*Marty Panzer*

Learn about publishing, copyright, and how to negotiate with record companies, agents, and managers. Be wary of long, drawn-out contracts. Seek the advice of an attorney if needed. First and foremost, see to it that your music is strong, honest, and clear in its intention. Learn how to negotiate a fee for clinics, recording situations, and live performances. Frequently you will be asked what your fee is. You don't want to aim too high or too low. I generally throw it back in the employer's court. Ask what they can handle and what they have paid to other comparable artists.
—*Bob Mintzer*

Make a professional-looking website and business cards, even if you don't like "networking." You want people to be able to get in touch with you after meeting you.
—*Alexa Tarantino*

👍 You must also be an entrepreneur. Define what success looks like to you. Create a long-term vision and the short-term steps to achieve it.

—*Rick Drumm*

Buy good quality equipment, and start saving money ASAP.—*David Arnay*

Create original music, and find outlets for it that generate residual income.—*Tim Kobza*

Don't ever give the rights up to any of your creative works or recordings.—*Maria Schneider*

👍 **Be a composer, and hang on to your publishing.**—Russ Ferrante

Be well prepared and willing to go the extra mile. It is personally rewarding, and it pays off.—*Marcio Doctor*

👍 **You don't need a manager to help you get gigs.**—*Christian McBride*

In business dealings, look for ways that all parties can benefit, but never let go of what you need.—*Cuong Vu*

You are running a Business! You are a small-business person! Your business is You! Some questions you need to find answers to:

- **Why should you be hired?**
- **What do you bring to a gig?**
- **What do you have to offer?**
- **What are your unique, different, and individual strengths?**
- **Are you prepared?**
- **Are you dependable?**
- **Can you be trusted?**—*Justin DiCioccio*

Keep a record of your income and expenditure from day one—and save in advance for the inevitable tax bill!
—*Christine Pendrill*

Get a good tax accountant.—*Tierney Sutton*

First, discover what you do that's special and unique. Then put your energy into honing and developing it. This will give people a reason to pay you for your art.
—*William Kanengiser*

Don't rely on others to handle your affairs; make sure you are at least looking over the shoulders of your manager, accountant, agent, etc.—*Gary Burton*

You never know when the bubble may pop, so try to save the best you can and do not live beyond your means.—*Leland Sklar*

Get your own gigs. Start your own band.—*Jim Payne*

Take every gig you can as a young musician, but don't sell yourself short. The experience you get from doing gigs cannot be taught in school.—*Matt Harris*

You can learn from any situation. Have gratitude, not an attitude. Positivity is an attribute.—*Adam Nussbaum*

Don't undercut yourself or others. Join the Musicians Union.—*Ed Soph*

Save early and often!—*Perry Dreiman*

Don't count your services short. If you don't stretch, no one will stretch for you.—*Scott Goodman*

You exist within a **professional ecosystem** *of INDIVIDUALS whose jobs, interests, and desires i n t e r s e c t with your own.*—Jeff Levenson

Follow the music honestly, not the money.—John Beasley

If you don't have the skills or feel comfortable negotiating, etc., then get a friend or agent/business manager with skills to help or work for you.—*Bob Barry*

Hone your music. Be aware of "business" details, but focus on the music. An imbalance of business and performing is never good. Focusing on the music (assuming you want to perform versus heading into business) will always open more business doors.
—John Clayton

Never leave your wallet in the dressing room.
—*Bob Becker*

Charles Fambrough once told me, "In the music business you only get job security by playing your butt off!"—John Ramsay

Save when you can. You may not always be regularly working.
—*Ralph Humphrey*

Know how to value your time.—*Jake Reed*

Be professional in every aspect of the music business.—Ignacio Berroa

When you go on a gig, always have a smile, and never look intimidated by players around you. Never call music contractors during lunch or dinner time. Take any gig; you never know who's in the audience.—*Joe Porcaro*

Know when to say, "No!"—*Joe Pereira*

It doesn't matter how hard you work at developing your musical skills if you do not learn how to "sell your product."—*Jeff Jarvis*

Being a musician is a lifestyle, not a business decision. Honor the music first, and leave no stone unturned.—Ed Carroll

If you work with someone (manager, etc.) who thinks it's okay to yell at you or any member of your team, then that someone needs to be fired.—*Mary Chapin Carpenter*

Invest as much as you can for retirement from every paycheck, and do not wait. Today, as hard as it is to admit, very few musicians can make a living without a second job. Prepare other skills, whether music related or not, to be able to make a living while pursuing your performance dreams.—Danny Gottlieb

Connect, connect, and connect! Who you know and who likes you are everything. People generally want to be around people with whom they feel a connection with. This is advice that is hard for me and that I'm still working on myself! Being comfortable onstage is easy for me, but being comfortable offstage is not.—*Alyssa Park*

Nothing lasts forever. Put something into savings for that rainy day when some producer or composer/arranger says, "Let's try that new kid!"—*Hal Blaine*

Be proactive. If you are waiting for the world to beat a path to your door, it will get lonely. If you have a hard time setting your price, get someone to represent you and do it for you.—*Shelly Berg*

Make, don't spend! Haha, of course you have to buy gear and food, etc. Bottom line for me is: I know that if I'm working, I'm making money. I leave all the other bill-paying stuff to someone I trust, i.e., a business manager or my better half.—*Will Lee*

Work on the music— if you play great people will find out about it.—*John Scofield*

You are your business. Find a good CPA that knows how to manage artists' finances. Always think in the long term when it comes to money.—*Benjamin Williams*

Get all agreements for service in writing, always. Use email, not text, for communication. Answer all important emails within 24 hours.—*Lynn Helding*

Report everything (income) to the IRS. Keep track of everything (mileage, receipts, and business-related expenses). They add up, and you'll feel better if you do. Be visible to others...out of sight, out of mind.—*Tim Ishii*

*Be smart about your finances. Spend what you can afford,
and buy only what you can pay off. When it comes to the
business of music, treat your fellow musicians fairly, and
pay those you hire fairly. Be someone everyone can respect.
It will pay you back many times over.*—Marvin Stamm

4 REASONS to take a gig:

BREAD,
HANG, MUSIC,
CAREER
DEVELOPMENT.

Gotta have three out of four.

Or, if one is music,

two out of four.

**If you're over 60,
axe the career development!**—Bill Cunliffe

Put 10 percent of your earnings away as savings as soon as you can.—Chuck Berghofer

**Be a player that everyone enjoys being around and who *always*
makes the band sound better. That's good business.**—Steve Houghton

*Be very, very good at at least one thing. Make sure people know
you're the best at that one thing. It's even better if you're very
good at three or four things.*—John Goldsby

**Vertical integration! Own everything you
create, top to bottom.**—Robin Meloy Goldsby

People with good intentions will always respect someone who represents themselves well, asks the right questions, and gets everything agreed upon in advance. The people who don't have your best interests in mind will try to avoid clarity when questioned by you. —Andy Newmark

And, perhaps, the best business advice for a musician to follow:

To polish, refine, and improve my own sound. —*Sadao Watanabe*

SOUND ADVICE

SECTION 7

Peter: I'll be brief for a change. Music has become too loud. Stage volumes are too loud because of inattention to monitor levels. (Typical scene during a soundcheck: "Why is the bass so loud in the trombones' monitors? Do you all need or want it *that* loud?" "NO." "Then somebody *please* pay attention and turn it DOWN!")

PA companies and sound (front-of-house and/or monitor) mixers have taken over control of our ability to hear and play with dynamics. The advent of the subwoofer has only made a bad problem WAY worse. A bass drum ought to sound like a bass drum—not like a howitzer cannon inside of your kitchen. Too much low-end is destroying the feel of the music. As funk-master Maceo Parker was heard saying to the sound man at a recent festival in Europe during his band's soundcheck (trying to get the guy to turn down the subs),

"The funk is not in the low-end."

Ladies and gentlemen of the jury: I rest my case.

Oh yeah, one more thing: horn players, learn to play the mic! You spend years developing a great sound, only to destroy it by jamming the mic into the bell of your horn?

And please think before you grab a live/hot mic to adjust it two inches, creating an ungodly loud noise that is amplified and blasts out of the PA speakers—that *was* a nice ballad you guys were playing.

PROBLEM: I can't hear the actual volume of my instrument when I'm wearing headphones.

SOLUTION: Pull the right or left headset off your ear, so that one ear is receiving the audio information from the headset, while the other ear is hearing the sound of your instrument in the room. Keeping the "pulled" headset side flush against your head will prevent any audio leakage from bleeding into your mics.

This is a trick or technique you can employ in the studio, sometimes for just a few seconds so you can reassure yourself of the "actual" or "pre-mic" sound your instrument is making in the studio environment.

TIP: It's always a good idea to invite the engineer out to the room and play a bit for him or her so they can hear what you sound like from where you are. That way, there's a reference point for expectations. You can do this onstage with front-of-house engineers as well. It's important to know what an instrument sounds like without the microphones (or, "without all of the assistance," as Buddy Rich once put it).

I've used in-ear monitors plenty of times. They can improve the stage sound as well as protect the hearing of the user. But they can also isolate the musician into his or her own universe, so that, while wearing them, I'm more apt to be in "Peter Land" versus in the spirit of the ensemble. It's a fine line between hearing everything you need to hear, and "How do I sound?" And that line can very easily become a musical Maginot Line.

How Do You Work with a Difficult Bandmember or Leader?

Peter: I've found myself in the hot seat over the years, working for various bandleaders (or under the baton of notoriously difficult conductors) who were *not* polite and were, on the contrary, demeaning and/or abusive. The question I always asked myself was, "Is there something I can learn from this ("this" meaning the person, band, or circumstance I was working with), and is it worth allowing it to play out? Most often the answer was yes, as in, "These people know a lot more about this stuff than I do, so I'm going to hang in there." Otherwise, I would not hesitate to call someone, *anyone*, out on rude or inappropriate behavior. However, this should be done with care and tact. My father taught me a valuable lesson when he advised, "You must always give something to someone before you attempt to take something else away." So, the obvious example is by beginning a conversation with a compliment and getting the other person to feel comfortable or, at least, not under attack. Gaining just a small amount of trust can really help level out the playing field so two people can then discuss a musical or personality issue without defensiveness or rancor.

No one plays badly on purpose, whether it's **you** or **the other**.

Music, like math, does not lie.

Strive for musical honesty, truth, and beauty. Be a diplomat, and know your worth. It is **okay to discuss your vision for the music**, even if that means directing a player to not play so damned much. Proceed at your own risk, however.

How Do You Make Suggestions and/or Tell a Bandmate to Turn It Down (Play Softer)?

Getting a musician to turn down an amp or monitor can be one of *the* most difficult things to accomplish.

Here's our advice:

If you're soundchecking, it's vital that you get the front-of-house PA turned *off* at some point so everyone can hear what the stage volume and balances are truly like.

The softer your stage volume, the better everything will sound out front. Period.

Someone needs to be the point person onstage regarding this. If you're a drummer, exercise your rights and leadership, as well as your unique seat in the "dynamics control department." Softer stage volume gives the band someplace to go dynamically, and it will sound better out front.

Volume is very much like a stack of dominoes—as soon as one element gets too loud onstage, everything will get out of whack pretty quickly.

Be polite (that, again) but firm.

If possible, record the music both onstage, as well as from the front of the house (i.e., the audience's point of view). You'll either get confirmation of what you suspect you hear happening, *or* you'll be surprised to learn that it actually sounds okay out front (or, horrors, that it's the drums that are too loud!).

The music does not lie. Sounds are not false, either—unless a sound person makes it so.

Here's one handy way to deal with bringing up a musical problem with a colleague, as illustrated by two contrasting approaches:

APPROACH #1: "I don't like what you're doing, so please change it." This will be met with resistance. After all, if someone said this to you, how would you feel?

APPROACH #2: "Hey, I apologize for the way that tune is feeling. I might be playing the wrong beat or hearing the music the wrong way" (i.e., playing too on top of the beat, behind the beat, busy, or simple). This will most often be met with a "thanks," plus a reassuring word that, no, you're not the only reason the song isn't working. **The other** will most likely add that he or she too is having some sort of problem (personal or musical). As soon as someone feels safe in an encounter, the more willing the person is to admitting to possible shortcomings or a misunderstanding.

People Skills Advice from the Pros

Music is something that comes out when you share it.—*Rita Marcotulli*

Be positive and care, even if the situation is not to your liking.—*Ralph Humphrey*

Treat others as you would want to be treated.—*Bill Platt*

Be pleasant, supportive, empathetic, optimistic, a good listener, and a team player.—*Bob Mintzer*

Be wise as a serpent and harmless as a dove.
—*Bruce Broughton*

Listen, listen, and listen some more, then reply.
—*Joe LaBarbera*

Never burn bridges.—*Satnam Ramgotra*

Don't send mixed messages.—*Ruth Price*

Try to be respectful and to learn something from everyone you come in contact with in your life!—*Emil Richards*

Being narcissistic or pretentious kills the joy of music. Being self-confident, yet kind and courteous to your partners in music, is a better way to make beautiful music.—*Cecilia Tsan*

Be considerate. Be kind to people and about people.—*Su-a Lee*

Be a good hang. Be respectful and allow people their quirks. Also, be aware of how your actions affect those around you. Be mindful of the shared space on the road.—*Damian Erskine*

Be kind.
—*Jake Reed*

Show up, keep up, and listen more than you talk.—*Perry Dreiman*

1.Think before you speak.
2. Don't assume you know it all (you don't).
3. Treat people the way you want to be treated.
4. Learn how to tell a joke very well (seriously).—*Jeff Ernstoff*

Be a good listener and read the room. Sometimes the best action is to be quiet and not offer an opinion unless asked. Remember important things. Show a genuine interest in other peoples' lives. Be respectful and show respect. It will come back to you.—*John DeChristopher*

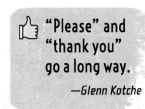

"Please" and "thank you" go a long way.
—*Glenn Kotche*

Treat others the way you would want them to treat you. Try to lift people up. Try to be a bright light (even if you are in a dark room). Try to be more like Louie Bellson: don't complain...the glass is half full...don't talk badly about people to make yourself look cool... try to learn from everyone and every player from every walk of life. In the words of our great friend and deep groove-playing bass legend Mike Porcaro: "Always have fresh breath."
—*Gregg Bissonette*

Be respectful in communications to all people associated with the biz of music. Journalists, fans, students, recording engineers, and fellow musicians can all be helpful down the road with that one connection you might need.—*Larry Koonse*

R.E.S.P.E.C.T. —*Bob Becker*

Be authentic and respectful.
—*Russ Ferrante*

[People skills] are more critical than you realize. There are plenty of people who play just as well. The only reason you'll get hired over them is because you are more pleasant to have in the room, more who play just as well...on the bus, or in the pit.
—*Don Carlin*

*Main thing is, do not make waves. Be pleasant to be
    around, and do not talk bad about anything or anyone.
You never know who is listening or who knows who. If
    people bring it up, just smile and be dismissive. Also
show up to gigs early, and offer to help others that
    need help.—Matt Howard*

Know how to say hello, goodbye, and thank you in the language
of whatever country you are going to; most of all be honest and
straight ahead with your hosts...no games.—David Liebman

 ## Listen without judgment.
—Carl Allen

**The Four Agreements:
    Don't take anything personally,
don't make assumptions,
    always do your best, and
be impeccable with your word.**
—Terri Lyne Carrington

**Embrace our differences. There is just *so*
much to absorb from others!—Charlie Bisharat**

Make everybody feel relaxed. Do it all as a team.—Jim Payne

**Do your best to help people you're with leave in a
better mood than when they met you.—Paul Wertico**

*Be reliable in your punctuality, in your playing, and in
your planning. That will go a long way towards getting
called again.—Jim Babor*

**Keep your sense of humor. Be kind
and a team player.—Tim Kobza**

When angry...take a beat. When criticizing or giving feedback, start
with the positive. Be kind.—Janis Siegel

The music business is a service industry. Be your own best rep.—George S. Clinton

Be friendly and support your colleagues.—John Beck

Be empathetic. Listen and care for others' needs as much as you would like yours to be met. Music-making is a team effort.
—Marcio Doctor

Send hand-written thank-you and follow-up notes whenever possible. People still love those—I know I do!
—Alexa Tarantino

Do your best to make every situation pleasurable for everyone involved. They'll never call you back if they have a bad recollection of your last encounter.
—Marty Panzer

 Be gracious and respectful, and welcome love, joy, and laughter as often as possible.—Matt Wilson

Listen to what others are saying. A true group dynamic, whether in an exchange of verbal or musical ideas, thrives when there is a "rotating chairperson-ship."
—Marc Copland

Respect and embrace each other.—Joe Lovano

There have been some great string quartets that were able to survive, even thrive, despite some famous personal conflicts, and play incredibly well together. I wonder if going out together for meals or cooking for each other could be therapeutic in some cases.—Pamela Havenith

If you can't just hang, and talking music is your only language, people are going to get bored of you quickly.—Scott Goodman

When in conversation, listen closely to what people are saying. —Steve Smith

The golden rule. Do unto others as you would like done unto you. You get what you give. —*Adam Nussbaum*

Be a good person.
Be a role model.
Stay humble. —*Jiggs Whigham*

Patience, understanding, humility—all go a long way in dealing with others. —Gary Burton

Don't talk too much—less is more. Nobody likes a complainer. —*Janet Paulus*

Try to remember the names of crew members, promoters, and stage hands out on the road. Be kind to them, and they will be kind to you.
—Allison Miller

I think being a good listener in any realm of your life may be the key to success. We know how important it is for the music. And, anybody who is married or in a relationship of any kind knows what a huge difference it can make! —*Jim Keltner*

 ### *Treat everyone with the same respect.*
—Joe Pereira

Do more listening than talking. —Joe Corsello
(NOTE: Joe Corsello went on to become a police detective for the Stamford, CT Police Department!)

Know thyself and, above all, be kind to each other. —*Rachel Z. Hakim*

Remember, you never know what the person you're talking to has lived through. Be generous. —Anne Hills

As Bruce Springsteen says, "Be steadfast, honest, and true." There is no other way to relate to people, in my opinion. —*Mary Chapin Carpenter*

Be nice to every client, your fellow musicians...
and **listen** first before you speak...also...**smile**.
—*Bernard "Pretty" Purdie*

People skills are as important as music skills. Music is a business of relationships—with your musical peers and with your audience. It takes empathy to be an artist, so it is a given that you have that trait. Make sure your empathy extends to those with whom you interact.
—*Shelly Berg*

I know it sounds corny, but you have to "work well with others."
—*John Scofield*

"It's nice to be important, but it's more important to be nice."—*Benjamin Williams*

Listen to what people have to say rather than for what you want to hear.—*Gary Motley*

Be the kind of person with whom others want to share the stage. Show up on time, being sober and appropriately dressed. Be ready to perform by being prepared. Be a team player, and the musicians you are working with will be moved to share the spotlight with you. I have certainly found this to be true in my career. Treat everyone with respect, and don't talk behind their backs. Be the kind of person you want others to be toward you. This formula will always be a winning one.—*Marvin Stamm*

Let people talk about themselves. Ask them questions.
—*Bill Cunliffe*

I've noticed for a long time that nice people work a lot more. It literally "pays" to be nice, and it's a lot more fun.—*Maria Schneider*

Be an effective communicator at every level.—*Steve Houghton*

Listen to other musicians. Listen to what they say, and listen to what they play.—*John Goldsby*

Advice "to and for" Drummers (Pun Intended) from the Pros

Drummers like to be in the driver's seat. It's in our nature, and it's this trait of wanting to take control of things that helps make us so important to any ensemble. This "taking charge" will often lead to a need to be first when and wherever a downbeat is played. This may manifest itself as being that first sound the listener hears when a new tempo or section of a piece occurs, such as the first note of an *a tempo* section after, say, an intro. So, imagine a quiet entrance where the bass and drums play the first note (the drummer is using brushes): FLAM.

Peter: I've gotten pretty good at "reading" the room when it comes to matching the entrance of the bass, complete rhythm section, or orchestra, and so on. But I'll be the first to admit that it's not always an easy thing to match and play at that exact moment when a bass player's finger plucks the string. Softly feathering a sizzle cymbal works. However, I've discovered a better way. Simply...**don't play!**

By this I mean have your brushes set on the snare drum, and let the bassist play the downbeat alone. *Then* come in playing time with the hi-hat on beat 2 (or play the 2 and 4 by accenting the brush/ride pattern on the snare). Et voilà...the listener hears a perfect downbeat, perfect because the bass has played it in total synchronism with their own instrument. No clutter, muss, or fuss. This is a counterintuitive approach to controlling the ebb and flow of the music, but this trick of surrender can work wonders in recording or orchestral settings. Try it.

Surrender in music does not mean that you're waving the white flag and giving up. On the contrary, the drummer is more able to pull the strings of the band by not always trying to muscle the music.

I'd like to pass along one other trick, something I figured out as a 13-year-old drummer playing my first vaudeville show in Atlantic City back in 1967. If the band director or conductor does not provide any sort of tempo indication by way of a count-off or visible upbeat, you can always play a cymbal crash on the downbeat and then glom onto whatever tempo consensus the band has quickly arrived at by the time the cymbal's sound has ebbed away. This is a total abdication of drumming responsibility, but it works in a pinch. In fact, this is similar to how many chamber music groups operate.

Now...here is some valuable advice for drummers—whether you're a drummer reading this book or someone who works with a drummer—from some of the best musicians we know.

Remember, you are the most important musician in the band, except for the leader, and even then it's often you who is responsible for the time feel, the dynamics, the interpretation of the music, the energy, everything. I always say, once I finish counting off the start of the song, the drummer becomes the bandleader. So, I always try to hire the best drummer I can get.
—*Gary Burton*

Play the room. —*Kait Dunton*

Learn how to sing. —*Kevin Lyman*

D Y **N A M I** C S !
—*Catina DeLuna*

There are few grooves worse than a drummer with one opinion and the bassist with the opposite opinion.
—*Antonio García*

Please practice on the downbeat...and use this thing they call a metronome.
—*George Garzone*

As a big band leader, I know the drummer is the most important player in the ensemble. A band is only as good as its drummer. I look for drummers who think like an arranger, who are cooperative, will take some direction, and, most importantly, prioritize the groove. It's gotta swing! —*Ellen Seeling*

Consistent "time" (like the drum corps), especially when playing "fills," should feel good to everybody, especially the bass player (smile)!—*Chuck Rainey*

> *To percussionists in general, as most of my work is orchestra: be considerate of harpists who need time to tune. We can't move our harps off the stage that easily, and it doesn't take more than 10 minutes max to do a good tuning in silence.—Janet Paulus*

Learn to play piano and write original music compositions and arrangements for all size groups and styles. Have a good understanding of theory outside the standard rudiments of drumming. Be a well-rounded "musician," not just a drummer, and more doors will open for you as you pursue a career in music.

—*Bart Marantz*

Listen to **the song,** and play to enhance the song. Same for all the players. It is not about imposing you on the song.—*Leland Sklar*

If you are a drummer, you are in the "feel-good" business, no matter what style you play. You maybe have tons of chops, but if your ride cymbal pattern, or your basic backbeat, or your shuffle, etc. doesn't feel good, it's not as desirable a musical situation to be connected with. Make sure that everything you play feels good!—*Andrew Rathbun*

I love drummers, and I'm glad to take advice from any drummer. As far as giving advice to drummers, I would say that often less is more. That applies to busyness and also volume.—*David Schwartz*

Listen to the soloist and each member of the group, and leave the ego at home.—*Tom Ranier*

Like the other musicians in a rhythm section, you are an accompanist. Your job is to make the music feel good and make everyone around you sound good. From a pianist's perspective: watch the volume in an acoustic situation. We can only play so loud. Ugh!—Matt Harris

When playing with a vocal group, be aware of your role as time-keeper. Different singers feel time differently, and it's hard enough negotiating that among the vocalists. As a solo singer, I look for the drummer to be more of a painter with time, while still keeping the ever-important groove.—*Janis Siegel*

Every drummer I've ever known, who isn't constantly vigilant about volume, is too loud. (If you can't understand and repeat the lyrics, you're too loud.) Singer's (and bassist's) corollary: Every singer and bassist I've ever known, who isn't constantly vigilant about intonation, is out of tune.—*Tierney Sutton*

You always have the green light with me playing... things can be toned down, but if the energy isn't there, it will not be found.—*David Liebman*

Choose your cymbals carefully so they are specific to the music you are playing and the ensemble you are part of.—*Alan Pasqua*

Pay attention to the bass player, and only solo if you have something to say.—*Dan Carlin*

Take the bass player out to dinner!—*Nathan East*

Don't play too loud.—*Perry Dreiman*

Make a beautiful sound; groove and feel trump chops by *a lot*.—*Russ Ferrante*

You are the bedrock of the group. Everything comes down to your feel and reliability. Being able to play groupings of 5 with your hands and groupings of 7 with your feet is neat, but if it doesn't fit the music, save it for the shed. If you lose the band and we can't all come in strong, nothing else really matters. It's music, not a dance battle.—*Damian Erskine*

When working with less-experienced musicians, rhythm-section players, or singers: be a good teacher when needing to clarify highly nuanced concepts like rhythmic subdivision, varieties of grooves, Latin styles and feels, "pocket," playing on top, playing behind, swing versus straight, etc. As a guitarist, I'm glad I had a few drummers in my life when I was young that set me straight on a few of these things.—*Tim Kobza*

To develop an approach beyond your instrument, follow the sound and create music within the music.—*Joe Lovano*

Don't overplay. "The most impressive form of power is restraint."—Thucydides
—*Jeff Ernstoff*

Try to climb inside the heads of the other musicians, in one way with the rest of the rhythm section, and in another way with the soloist. With the rhythm players, listen first and engage in a conversation, suggesting and responding, rather than monopolizing the musical direction. With the soloist, listen first; do your best to feel you and the soloist are one and that you are playing along with him or her; stay close to see/feel where the soloist is going. By doing so you can accompany in the most sympathetic way.—*Marc Copland*

Always serve the song, and be able to offer a clear sound at any dynamic level.—*Matt Wilson*

Don't forget your sticks.—*Marty Panzer*

Have some basic skills with at least one other musical instrument.
—*Claus Hessler*

Think like an architect. Provide the foundation and overall structure, and make good use of space and contrasting materials in order to provide clarity and a safe environment.—*Marcio Doctor*

If you can't hear the melody, you're playing too loud!—*George S. Clinton*

Learn to play with intensity at all dynamic levels, especially soft. And, to play all styles.—*John Beasley*

Be sensitive.—*Su-a Lee*

Do not play like a mad man or woman during a break when people are trying to give a break to their ears.—*Cecilia Tsan*

Help the band, help the band, and help the band. **Talk** to anyone you're playing with if there are playing issues that need addressing. If I can't talk to them, I can't play with them.—*John Clayton*

Forget democracy—the whole band doesn't need a solo in each tune.—*Ruth Price*

Less is more (not always, but for me, most of the time!).—*Alexa Tarantino*

The advice I generally give to student drummers concerns keeping a solid foundation (hi-hat on 2 and 4 in a big band setting), utilizing the right amount of groove versus acknowledgement of band figures, not over-playing, underplaying, and playing fills that don't disrupt flow and groove.—*Bob Mintzer*

Listen, and play in time, please. Also, don't be afraid to play soft.—*Grant Geissman*

Keep time, stay in the moment, make it feel good, and listen!—*Tim Weston*

Making music is a team sport—a conversational art. We are all there to serve the music. A band will only go as far as the drummer is going to take them. This remains true today. I love the drums and drummers!—*Steve Khan*

Simplify! There are a lot of parts to a single beat. Playing in the wrong part doesn't feel good to the rest of us. Many good horn players DO have good time, so let us "play" with you. There is melody/music, and there are "chops." They aren't the same.—*Liesl Whitaker*

Besides being simple, be easy, be musical, and groove your butt off. Figure out how to express all of your ideas and intentions, without losing good time, intensity, or drama, at *pianissimo.*—Cuong Vu

Learn to have a "thick skin." Good conductors will talk to you more than anyone in the band. They know that if the drummer gets it, the band will follow.

—*Jeff Jarvis*

My advice to drummers is the same as I give to myself and everyone in the band. Start by playing less than what your instincts are probably telling you to do. Collaboration happens in that space you leave.—*Shelly Berg*

Make sure you can
hear **everyone** else.—*Bill Cunliffe*

Find **your** 2 and 4. There's so much strength in the way a drummer lays down a backbeat when they have decided where they want it to be. Own it. Notice who's out there working. All of those people have a way of laying it down that helps the story to be told, but it's also done with a voice that's truly their own. Drumming is a service industry. Those who are working the most seem to have discovered that groove is what gets you hired. Serve the music as best you can! Know your instrument well enough that you can make **listening** a priority. That really helps you be in it!—*Will Lee*

Learn some piano. Enjoy the songs!—*John Scofield*

Always watch the piano player for cues!—*Gary Motley*

The drums and cymbals are instruments of color as well as those of time-keeping. Always make sure your colors fit the picture the ensemble and/or soloists are trying to paint. Listen for the music that is being made rather than always relying on the notes on the paper. Regardless of the need for the visual aspect of the music, the aural aspect is most important. As expressed above, be a team player. Play **with** your musical cohorts, not at them.—*Marvin Stamm*

Get a good sound out of the drums!—*Benjamin Williams*

I would encourage a drummer to learn how to play each song *without* cymbals. It enhances a drummer's entire perspective on each voice in the trap kit and how they can be used to **enhance** the composition. Too often I feel the novice drummer has a "knee jerk" reaction with cymbals, and this can help break that habit.—*Joe Deal*

My favorite drummers are always listening and always open to letting the music flow in any given direction at any given time. They are also well rounded stylistically and can play any musical feel with authenticity. They play with dynamics and can sight-read perfectly. And sometimes they bring their own drums and don't charge for cartage!—*Gordon Goodwin*

I'll leave room for you. Please return the favor!—*Jeff Dalton*

Lead the ensemble in time, and blend your sound as needed.
—*Raynor Carroll*

Listen to everyone else playing, and support them as best you can. There is a delicate balance to interjecting and responding to a soloist's ideas and stepping on their ideas with your response. That fine line is what we call taste. Play with a wide dynamic range. If you are truly listening, it will happen naturally.—*Chris Brubeck*

Learn harmony and play piano.—*Steve Houghton*

Never underestimate the power (and beauty) of brushes.—*Robin Meloy Goldsby*

Be able to play **time.**—*Joe Corsello*

Always believe in yourself. Also, from Ed Soph—learn to play the bass drum pedal heel down.—*John Robinson*

Always take your time before each song to choose the perfect tempo for the song. Or, better yet, buy a Tama Rhythm Watch, and write down on the set-list the perfect tempos for each song. Then listen to that tempo and get it into your soul before you start each song.—*Gregg Bissonette*

It's all about touch. Think touch rather than hit, and your playing will automatically be more musical.—*Bill Platt*

To drummers on soloing: Play from the melody, and let your first musical statement carry you through.—*Allison Miller*

SECTION 8   FROM A TEACHER'S PERSPECTIVE

From My Own Teaching Archives ...

No one is interested in hearing a solo—they're interested in hearing a story.

Investigate the Alexander Technique and how it applies to your instrument—playing posture. No more scrunching or tilted-head playing!

Authenticity versus showmanship—is there a middle ground?

To a non-drummer: You can always ask yourself, "What would George Garzone do?" (I think he'd know the tune.) The "fail" on the post-drum-solo-entrance can only be attributed to your not being in the musical moment. By that I mean you should be singing the form to yourself during any bass or drum solo, etc., and be "there" so you know where everything is. This helps to make for an enlightened and aware bandstand.

Most important for **you, as an artist,** is to know *specifically* what it is you want and need to say. But it's okay to take your time finding this out...I'm still working on it.

Staying **true** requires **trust**. You must trust the music. You must trust the other players. Most of all, you must *trust yourself*.

As far as adding time to a band or prerecorded track, as soon as you try to play a "beat," you're thinking **vertically**, and, if the lines don't line up, it gets ugly fast. However, if you think **horizontally**, the music flows, and everyone can have a good time.

Comparing two approaches: one seems to stay in a more or less constant state of tension, while the other arrangement utilizes tension and release throughout. Tension/release ultimately gives a piece of music more impetus and is more inviting to any listening audience. Why? Any story needs both elements...too much of one without the other forms its own version of monotony (no matter how sophisticated)...granted, this is a matter of personal taste.

That being said, think of the heart beating. It's all tension and release that serves or functions to pump the blood and life force—something to think about. My suspicion or impression is that some of us lean towards tension as a modernistic device. Every age has its own tension, I suppose.

Brushes—Student: "I can't play brushes" = **wrong mindset!**

It's **all music.** *Just play*—don't set yourself up for anything other than **musical success** whenever you play in whatever circumstance!

When you approach it with concentration, commitment, focus, and **belief,** you *can* and *will* play just about anything you set your mind to. And when you're working with other musicians, you *need* to make that commitment! And, you sounded great when you forgot about technique but stayed within the constraints we agreed upon (that were imposed, actually). Restrictions or limitations *help* the creative process. Learn to use them in your everyday playing situations!

GAME RULES: What am I going to outlaw or deny to myself as an option so I can discover something new, and not risk sounding like the 16-year-old version of myself?

Limitations are nearly the same thing as **disciplined choices**—restricting your licks diet will make you come up with new stuff!

And the **secret** to brush playing (or most stick playing for that matter) is that you do not need to play as fast as you might think you do.

Don't sweat the small stuff. Don't rock the boat. And, never lean sideways in a canoe.

Meanwhile, our friend and colleague, drummer and author Steve Houghton, sent us the following quotes he has been heard to say in his Jacobs School of Music teaching studio at Indiana University. Steve is way more succinct than we are.

Immerse yourself in the music.

With structure comes freedom.

Practice with performance intensity.

Serve the music—be selfless.

It's not about **you**; the music flows through you.

50 percent concept—50 percent technique.

Play the room.

Tripletize.

Dig deep.

No preconceptions about the music—be open.

Transcriptions

Peter: You're playing many of the notes "right," but nothing is sounding or seeming or feeling like that musician. You must share some of your practice time with something I'll call **fantasy time**, where you're allowed to make mistakes but you are always searching for the right **sound** and **feel** of the player whose work you're learning or trying to emulate. I recommend that you do this during every practice session (ninety minutes or two hours or one hour or five minutes)!

One problem I have with transcriptions is that they often sacrifice the intent of the musician who created the original solo by over-notating a rhythmic phrase. In other words, I'm fairly certain that Coleman Hawkins or Elvin Jones were not consciously thinking of a 7:6 phrase—it's just how the notes came out! Maybe my problem is not with transcribers so much as it is with our fixed system of music notation. That said, it's better than nothing!

Speaking of Elvin—my other problem with the art of transcribing and practicing and performing is the same problem I have with most everyone (including myself) who tries to sound like Elvin. The only way you will really sound like Elvin is to play from something resembling the source of why he played that way, but not with the perceived physicality or volume because it inevitably always comes out too hard and somehow quite wrong.

ADVICE: In your transcription and performance, figure out how to achieve **intensity** without too big of a volume jump or onslaught. When practicing any transcription, don't get frustrated...hang in there. I suggest you **isolate** one bar at a time and play it over and over, and then expand the region (before and after) until you **own** all of those passages. *Any* hiccup must be dealt with this way in order for you to truly own the piece.

I recommend you play some of the solo **by ear** (any isolated part will do). Don't be shy to try even a half-measure quote, etc....similar to trying to impersonate a famous person's voice (try it!). This will make the actual transcribing process go more quickly and smoothly, and help it become more energizing.

I'll admit, I came to the transcription party late in life—I always tried learning the gist and essence of someone's playing by ear (and not always with the best results). We find transcriptions to be an invaluable learning tool here at the Thornton School of Music Jazz Studies Department at USC.

A Personal Story

In Case of Emergency, Don't Break My Glass

You know that moment in a movie when the main character senses that something is amiss, and there's an asynchronous blip? Like when the time-space continuum has just been veered off course a teeny bit due to some small percentile of cosmic mischief. This moment usually serves as an indicator that something is about to happen. Right? And you know when *you* have experienced something similar, and you either pay attention to it or you don't? And, if you don't, it's usually because you receive the signal but you don't understand it or know what to do with it. How to **process** that cosmic hint. All otherwise known as honoring your instinct. Or listening to your gut. Paying attention.

Well...you should certainly listen to credible advice. Like when people tell you that leaving your drums in the car is a bad idea. How many times have you heard or read that? Plenty, I bet. We have, too.

Peter: I experienced that blip a while back when I tipped the bellman of a hotel's valet parking lot to watch the car. I was grooving on the high of having played a great concert and knowing that I was about to enjoy a good night's sleep. Felt the blip but paid it no heed. Only to hear the hotel room telephone ring a short while later with a voice intoning, "Mr. Peter, your car has been broken into..." And, that stomach-sinking feeling rushing down the hall to the elevator and running outside to see your car's rear window smashed into a thousand pieces and *not* seeing all your drums where they had been snugly resting just twenty minutes earlier. Scanning the damage and assessing what was there and what wasn't, the first thing I noticed was that my cymbals *were* there, and I said out loud, "Okay...I can deal with everything else." The loss amounted to all my drumset's hardware, a prototype snare drum made for me by Tama, and a small suitcase filled with video gear. The biggest loss there was the film I had made only hours earlier with the band...I thought it was the best solo I had ever played. My "fish that got away" story... it was huge.

So, the next day I spent dealing with the insurance company for the damage done to the car and getting the window replaced. My wife and I still had quite a drive to the next town for that night's pair of shows and managed to make it to the venue just in time for a quick soundcheck and dinner. A drummer had set up the club's house drums, and I jumped onto the kit, grateful for his help and also looking forward to making music out of what had been a pretty lousy day. I noticed that the drums were elevated quite a bit higher than I normally play, but I treated it as if I were sitting in and didn't give it a second thought. A different blip.

Show time. The gift of music. Connecting with my musical friends. Connecting with my cherished cymbals, using borrowed drumsticks, and playing on an unknown kit at a new elevation. This is the kind of "high" I like. I felt totally free. The drums were also spread out more than usual for me. It all felt like a gift, somehow. *This* was the best I had ever played. Or at least it seemed like it.

The theft provided an opportunity for me and my wife to go into married-action-mode. Team spirit kicked in. There wasn't time, need, or motivation for any recriminations (although I apologized several times for being a knucklehead in the first place). We functioned as one. My friends all chipped in with support, drumsticks, drum setting-up, and so on. The music showed up and gave me strength and happiness. The loss was a gift! I saw new possibilities for playing. I learned a lot.

The stolen stuff? Showed up a few weeks later at a music store when a young couple strolled in schlepping my two hardware bags and that snare drum. While the store clerk tried to find the drum on a computer for a purchasing price, these two fencers got spooked, grabbed the drum, and abruptly left, with my hardware sitting abandoned on the shop floor. The drum will probably wind up in a garbage bin, but I hope not. I really hope that someone will be able to play on it and benefit from what the drum might tell them. And what they will hear? Depends on if they're paying attention.

SECTION 9 · NON-PERFORMANCE CAREERS IN MUSIC

Is a College Degree Still Valuable?

Dave: I've been asked this question many times over the years, and the answer is "yes" for the following reasons.

- Many skills you acquire while earning a degree will be useful in other fields outside music.

- Pursue what you love and not what you think will pay the most.

- If you're really passionate about a performance career, then go for it.

- Set a timeframe to reach your goal (five to seven years), and then move on.

- Have a plan B in place.

- There are more options available to you with a music degree than without. Teaching is one of the most common careers in music.

- Because many musicians typically combine multiple jobs with multiple income streams to support themselves and their families, a college degree can be most beneficial.

- Some careers require graduate education (such as college-level teaching and conducting) or additional training beyond what you'll find in an undergraduate program.

- Entrepreneurial skills, the ability to use the latest relevant technology, and basic business skills such as marketing, are also useful both inside and outside of music.

- Keep your eyes and ears open to the ever-changing opportunities created by technology. New avenues for consuming/creating music, innovative products, new teaching methods, and the use of music as a therapeutic tool all translate to new career options in a rapidly changing music world.

Creating a Music Industry Resume

Dave: The purpose of a resume is to get an interview or audition. Since it is usually the first glimpse/impression of you someone will see, it is very important that it includes the right information. Though it may not always feel like it, most people are looking for reasons to accept, not reject your résumé. Below is a basic guide to help you create your own résumé.

1. Because a résumé is a marketing tool and not a history of your life and career, think carefully about what to include and what to leave out. The content should only include information that is relevant to the position you are seeking. You may need to refine your résumé many times until it best represents both you and your accomplishments.

2. Try to keep your résumé to one page. Because someone may only look at your résumé very quickly, make sure it's organized and succinct.

3. Make sure everything is spelled correctly, that the content is formatted the same way, and that the fonts you choose are clean and easy to read.

4. Have your résumé updated (with any new experiences) and ready at all times so you can respond quickly if an opportunity comes your way.

5. To start, include your name, music name (if applicable), instrument (if applicable), and your contact information at the top of the résumé.

6. If you are a recent graduate, list your education details at the top of the résumé. If you already have several years of music performance experience under your belt, your education details can appear at the bottom.

7. The area of music in which you're heading (performance, teaching, music industry, etc.) will determine the experiences and background information you include on your résumé. Be sure to organize the information in terms of your strengths and how they relate to the specific skills and job you're applying for.

8. Start with your most recent experiences/accomplishments first.

9. Do not include false or exaggerated information, as this will most likely come back to haunt you.

10. References from teachers, players, and/or composers can be helpful if they are from prominent and respected people in the music community, and will give your résumé strength.

11. List only those ensembles/experiences that best represent your experience to date and how they relate to the specific job you're applying for. Do not list everything you've ever done to try and make your résumé look more impressive.

12. When listing awards and honors, include only important competitions, scholarships, and/or honors achieved in college, graduate school, or vocational school. Do not include high school awards and activities.

13. Make sure your cover letter is professional, courteous, short and to the point, and relevant to the application you're applying for. Again, use good grammar and check for spelling errors.

RESUMÉ: RECENT GRAD

JANE DOE

Phone
Email
Website

PROFILE SUMMARY

- Wide-ranging editorial experience in journalism and publishing, serving as writer, editor, proofreader, and interviewer.
- Proficiency in music composition, orchestration, and classical piano performance.
- Extensive skills in score and parts preparation using notation software.
- Broad range of administrative skills, developed through editorial positions and music and film internships.

EDUCATION

Berklee College of Music, Boston, MA   2006—2008
Professional Diploma: Film Scoring; Instrument: Piano
Magna Cum Laude
Awards: Berklee World Scholarship Tour Award Recipient, 2006-, 2007
          Berklee Achievement-Based Scholarship Award Recipient, 2007-, 2008

EXPERIENCE

Apr 2009 –
Jan 2010

WRITER

JezebelMusic.com, Brooklyn, NY
An online music magazine that provides reviews, commentary, and local artist profiles.
Wrote columns highlighting artists' musicianship. Interviewed upcoming local bands about their origins, writing process, and performances. Contacted musicians or band managers directly to schedule interviews. Liaised between interviewees and photographer to set up photo shoots.

Jun 2006 –
Dec 2008

EDITORIAL ASSISTANT/PROOFREADER

Berklee Press, Boston, MA
Proofread text, music notation, and audio recordings at all stages of production, on dozens of instructional books, CDs, and DVDs. Created and edited music notation using Finale. Performed various administrative tasks for Managing Editor.

Nov 2008 -
Present

FREELANCE COMPOSER

Reel Braveri, New York, NY
Reel Braveri is an artist collective that supports creative projects amongst its members.
Edited music to picture for five of nine episodes to a two-hour web-series using MX tracks from previous episodes. Provided original music when appropriate. Worked with director, previous composer, and sound editor during process.

RESUMÉ: PROFESSIONAL

John Doe
Percussionist and Educator

Address
Phone
Email

Education
University of California, Los Angeles
MM Percussion Performance
June 2017

Azusa Pacific University
BM Percussion Performance
Mathematics Minor
May 2014

Performance Experience
Section Percussionist   2017 - Present
Pasadena Community Orchestra – Pasadena, CA

Percussion Substitute   2017 - Present
American Youth Symphony – Los Angeles, CA

Section Percussionist   2017 - 2018
South Coast Symphony – Aliso Viejo, CA

Percussionist   November 2017
Los Angeles Opera Company – Los Angeles, CA

Principal Timpanist   2014 - 2016
Young Musicians Foundation Debut Orchestra – Los Angeles, CA

Teaching Experience
Percussion Coach   2018 - Present
Blair High School – Pasadena, CA

Drum-line Coach   2015 - Present
Maranatha High School – Pasadena, CA

References Available
Upon Request

The Interview

Dave: If a playing career doesn't pan out or if you're looking to make a change, there are many areas of the music business you can pursue. Some of these options include music manufacturing, music publishing, music retail, teaching at a school/university level, etc. When applying for a job in one of these areas, chances are you will most likely have to interview for the position. As someone who has interviewed many people over the years, here are some general pointers to help you get through the process and be your best.

Before the Interview

1. Read the job description thoroughly so you understand what the job entails.

2. Your performance in an interview will most likely be based on the thoroughness of your research and how well prepared you are. So, do your homework and learn some detailed information about the company (history and philosophy, products, reputation, management talent/style, etc.).

3. Make sure your résumé is concise, that it addresses the job you're applying for, that everything is spelled correctly, and that you've used proper grammar.

4. Research similar companies and/or schools so you have an idea of what the pay structure is for a job with similar responsibilities.

During the Interview

1. Because your attire/appearance is important in creating that first impression, you'll need to dress appropriately for the interview, even if you know that the employees may dress casually. For men, we suggest a suit (sport coat) and tie, and something comparable for women.

2. Give yourself plenty of time to arrive at your scheduled appointment in case something goes wrong (a flat tire, wrong directions, an accident on the freeway, a lane closure, etc.).

3. Wait for the interviewer to take a seat first before sitting down.

4. Make sure you're relaxed and in control, that you're speaking clearly, that you sound natural and not over rehearsed, that your legs and arms aren't crossed, and that you make proper eye contact.

5. Smile.

6. At the start of the interview, thank the interviewer for the opportunity to meet.

7. Don't be afraid to ask questions during the interview.

8. At the close of the interview, it's okay to ask how soon they intend to make a decision and whether you should follow up with them or whether they will reach out to you.

9. Thank the interviewer, and shake hands if the situation allows.

After the Interview

Send a brief thank-you note when you return home after the interview— or the following day at the latest.

Alternate Careers in Music

Aside from pursuing a performance career, there are many other options available within the music industry. Some of the more popular career options include music publishing, music engraving, music retail, recording, music licensing, non-profit management within a music organization, personal assistant, copyediting, teaching, music therapy, composing/arranging, copyright administrator, music librarian, studio engineer, etc. Keep your options open! Music will always be in your life.

How Do I Submit a Manuscript for Publication Consideration?

Dave: As someone who has reviewed hundreds of manuscripts over the years, I have seen, heard, and/or edited just about every kind of publication. When soliciting a manuscript or piece of music to a potential publisher, here are some basic points to consider:

- Make sure you're sending your manuscript to a music publisher. You'd be surprised at the number of non-music books we've received over the years.

- Do some research to see if there's something similar already on the market.

- If your subject matter is similar to something already on the market, explain how your book/approach is different.

- If you're unsure of what type of new books the publisher is looking for, contact them to ask.

- Include audio and/or video components with your book, composition, or arrangement.

- Manuscripts should be addressed to the proper department and/or editor.

- If sending a printed copy for review, please include a self-addressed, stamped envelope for the manuscript's return. Manuscripts lacking return postage are usually discarded.

- Most of the major publishers ask that you allow approximately 8–12 weeks for a reply.

- Do not send your only copy to the publisher.
- Do not send your manuscript to a publisher if it's currently being reviewed by another publisher.
- Submissions should be original material.
- Please keep in mind that a rejection isn't always a reflection of the quality of the manuscript submitted. Many times it has to do with the fact that a publisher may already have something similar in their catalog, or they don't publish the type of material being submitted.

Dave: I'm a good example of someone who started their career in one area of music but switched to another, equally satisfying one that checked off all the boxes. I received a percussion performance degree (with a minor in composition) because that had always been my passion and how I thought I would make my living. After being on the road for a few years, however, I didn't like the "road life." It wasn't the playing, but the constant traveling, setting up and tearing down equipment, being away from home for long periods of time, and the uncertainty of when the next lucrative road gig would come along (or if anything would come along at all). After a while, the pressure and uncertainty of all that made me rethink my options and how I could best utilize the skills and knowledge I already had. Music publishing ended up checking all the boxes, as it offered not only a stable job and income but the opportunity to be creative/inventive, a chance to influence the direction of music publishing, the opportunity to compose music and write/edit books used by hundreds of thousands of music students all over the world, and an additional income stream in the form of royalties. I have never regretted that decision, and I am thankful for the platform it has given me to share and help others find direction and meaning in their own career path. In retrospect, knowing what I know now, I would have started studying piano, music theory, and composition at an earlier age.

Here are some thoughts from the pros about what they would have done differently in their studies and/or careers. The most common responses included improving piano skills, studying composition, and practicing more or differently. We've included a sample of those answers from our contributors as well as the more unique or general responses below.

What's Something You Would Have Done Differently?

Piano

I would have studied piano more seriously and really made it a point to play. —Tierney Sutton

I wish I did not stop playing piano when I began with the cello. —Cecilia Tsan

Learning to play the piano and arranging. —Ignacio Berroa

I would have pursued more solo piano skills and better vocal technique as a younger person—I came late to the party! —Jennifer Barnes

Would not have stopped studying classical piano when I was in high school. —Matt Harris

I would have taken piano lessons. Or guitar. —Abbie Conant

As a guitarist, I wish I had spent more time early on studying— and practicing—piano. —Grant Geissman

In my studies I would have spent more time learning piano and drums. As a performer on a single note wind instrument, I realize more and more how little I know about harmony and rhythm. —Tim Ishii

I would have worked more diligently at acquiring piano skills. One needs piano skills to compose/arrange, to teach, to demonstrate—everything! —Jeff Jarvis

Composition

I would have formally studied composition.—*Allison Miller*

> I would have gotten deeper into composition
> and orchestration.—*Tim Kobza*

Studied arranging and composition.—*Damian Erskine*

I would have studied composition and orchestration
in more depth in college.—*Ivan Hampden, Jr.*

I definitely would have studied arranging and
composition. I was too impatient to just sing.—*Janis Siegel*

**Studied arranging for large ensembles. I am committing to it right
now, though. Never too late, right?—*Matt Wilson***

Study more counterpoint and orchestration in college.—*Otmaro Ruíz*

Practice

Practiced so much more.—*George Garzone*

I would have made more efficient use of my practice time!—*Steve Khan*

> *I wish I had practiced with more deliberate
> focus when I was younger.*—*Liesl Whitaker*

*I wish I had realized how quickly I needed to make a living after
I got out of high school and been more dedicated to practicing in
those years when I was still living with my parents.*—*Larry Koonse*

**Practiced more and worried less about what
others thought. (Wait, that's two things.)**—*Neil Percy*

I'd have practiced more when I was a student
and had not only the time but also the guidance.—*Christine Pendrill*

**I wish I had practiced more and
asked more questions.**—*Benjamin Williams*

Practiced more intelligently and analytically.—*John Clayton*

General

*Really discover J. S. Bach and Louis Armstrong earlier! Other than that,
the fate gods have usually been very kind to me.*—*Jiggs Whigham*

Taken a course in conducting.—*Gary Burton*

Never doubted my own potential or anyone else's.
—*John Daversa*

When I was beginning to play percussion in my
school band, I began to keep a diary of all the
interesting things that happened. I wish I had
continued this diary throughout my life and used
it as a way to hone my writing skills. The ability
to write succinctly and coherently is one of the
most valuable skills a musician can develop.
—*Russell Hartenberger*

Learn to play more instruments! I still can!
—*Matt Howard*

**I wish I hadn't deterred myself
(as a female) from studying conducting.**
—*Michelle Makarski*

Learn how to play drums and sing at the same time.
Sorry if that's two things.—*Perry Dreiman*

I would have liked to have studied with more teachers.
—*Scott Goodman*

Gone to school and gotten a proper music education.
—*Russ Ferrante*

Studied more foreign languages.—*Bob Becker*

**I would have been more efficient with my time:
Quality versus Quantity.**—*Kenny Aronoff*

**Not quit Miles Davis's band because of a personal
situation. Not given up on being a film composer at 30.**
—*John Beasley*

Studied jazz harmony. —*Su-a Lee*

I started my music studies when I was six years old. I wish that I would have
started asking music questions earlier in my studies!—*Emil Richards*

*I would have been more outgoing in who I met
and what I studied.*—*Bruce Broughton*

I am happy with how my studies and career have gone. In conservatory
I did a good deal of orchestral and chamber music playing, learning how
to function in ensembles and perform with some level of consistency.
I studied jazz on my own and played and hung out outside of school. I
would have liked to have studied with a classical composition teacher,
but playing in ensembles and doing intensive listening to classical music
were the next best thing.—*Bob Mintzer*

**I would have made more of an effort
to study business and entertainment law.**—*John Ramsay*

Actually, I don't like to think in terms of what I could have done differently
in the past, since, just like when performing music: **1.** It's too late to change what
you've already done or played. **2.** Sometimes "mistakes" turn out better than you
[would've] imagined. **3.** I'm happy and grateful for my life as it is, so changing
anything in the past may also have changed where I've ended up—perhaps for the
better, but also possibly for the worse.—*Paul Wertico*

I wish I had studied solfège at an early age.—Joe Porcaro

I would have focused/concentrated solely on being a player rather than branching out into other areas of the music business.—Tim Weston

Learn more about recording technology and composition skills while in college.—*Terri Lyne Carrington*

I would have kept some of my feelings to myself and not taken things personally (while not allowing myself to forget).—Carl Allen

Instead of rushing towards the "goals," I would have looked for the easiest, most simple things I couldn't do, and started from there, chipping away at it slowly and thoroughly.—Cuong Vu

Haha! Way too much to name here. But I probably would have given my classical studies more attention. My **arco** playing should be better than it is.
—*Christian McBride*

Learn more about the financial side of the business at an early age.
—*Rick Drumm*

I would have focused on score study and conducting rather than simply playing the trumpet. Gaining objective knowledge rather than massaging my subjective self.—*Ed Carroll*

Grown up sooner, not have been so emotional, and trusted my intelligence.—Anne Hills

I would've compared myself less to others.—Gary Motley

I wish I had been kinder, less critical of my younger self. To me, the biggest gift that comes with the wisdom of age is letting go of the tyranny of perfectionism, recognizing and accepting that it's not possible to be perfect. But my younger self had to suffer through that. And it is so freeing to know oneself so well as we get older; it allows us to do our best, most honest work.—*Mary Chapin Carpenter*

I would have studied with additional older and legendary drummers.—Danny Gottlieb

Not spent so much time and energy being unnecessarily hard on myself. In hindsight, had I known how helpful a good therapist could be, I would have had less anguish in my life and possibly more success earlier in my career. Despite it all, I am truly humbled and honored to be where I am today. To be actively involved in such an incredible music scene as the one that fills my life with creative friends and inspiring moments that pay my bills, not to mention an incredible family life, is a large miracle on many levels.—*Ingrid Jensen*

I wish I had transcribed more solos when I was teenager.
—*Ethan Iverson*

Listened to more (and varied) music, which is hard to do while you're shedding for the next gig all the time.—*Will Lee*

I would have learned the business much earlier and kept my mouth shut!—*Bernard "Pretty" Purdie*

Learned to do things without caring what others thought or set an impossible bar for myself only to sabotage myself. Don't do that. If you want to learn piano for example, learn it for yourself; don't shoot yourself in the foot with the excuse that you'll never be as good as Keith Jarrett. Just do it anyway.—*Vinnie Colaiuta*

I would have paid more attention to habitual muscle tensions and imbalanced positions before they became engrained.—*William Kanengiser*

I would've studied business in college and aimed to understand music business and law early in my career.—Joe Deal

Believed in myself more. *And*, found a mentor earlier.—*Bill Cunliffe*

Would have studied film scoring and gone for that career.—*Kenny Werner*

I would have gotten a master's degree and pursued a full-time college position. As much as I love teaching, adjunct positions are, shall we say, less than ideal.—*Fred Simon*

Compose more.—*Alan Pasqua*

Left a bad teacher sooner.—*Lynn Helding*

I shouldn't have worried so much about everything.—*Kristin Korb*

I would have made a point to personally get to know many more of my musical heroes—they're just people, too!—*John Goldsby*

SECTION 10 : THE WORLD'S GREATEST ADVICE

We posed two general questions to over 150 of the world's most renowned jazz, classical, and rock/pop instrumentalists, educators, engineers, composers/arrangers, singers, songwriters, and teachers. The first, "What's the best advice you've ever received?, followed by "What's the best advice you've ever given?" As you read through the answers below, we think it will become obvious why this section is called "The World's Greatest Advice."

The Best Advice I've Ever Received

Listen to yourself when you play—get past the stress of getting out the notes.—*Janet Paulus*

Work your butt off and the sky's the limit. You can achieve anything with the right attitude and hard, hard work! Also, listen!— to all kinds of music—**a lot!**
—*Matt Harris*

Sing when you play.—*Rita Marcotulli*

Move forward and don't look back.
—*George Garzone*

Practice playing slowly.—*Catina DeLuna*

Do what you love.
—*Charlie Bisharat*

Develop a positive attitude! Turn around a **negative situation**, and **make it positive!**
—*Justin DiCioccio*

Be on time, pay attention, and be involved. Treat each project like it is your project.—*Leland Sklar*

Play the truth, which means to have intention behind every note. Don't play something unless you really mean it.
—*Glenn Kotche*

**From Shelly Manne: Let the drummer
be in charge of the time feel.**—*Gary Burton*

While you're working hard to develop your skills, don't forget why you fell in love with music in the first place. Stay connected to music that **moves** you and not just the music that someone else tells you that you "should" like!—*Jennifer Barnes*

**Play the *music* at hand.
What does it tell you to play? Listen!**
—*Adam Nussbaum*

Breathe.—*Alan Pasqua*

After a long week of rehearsals of African drumming and the music of Steve Reich, a student bounded into my studio and said, "I've got it! I know what it all means! Subdivide and conquer!" For me the phrase "subdivide and conquer" is not only a great way to think about rhythm, but it is also an aphorism that can be applied to many things in life.—*Russell Hartenberger*

Follow and live your excitement and passions.
—*John Daversa*

Try to remember it's **all** a choice and
a learning experience.—*Skip Hadden*

1. The idea of "success" is a mirage. Embrace the process of what you are doing instead of focusing on the results. The process of learning, composing, practicing, and studying is what is important. If you embrace that, everything else will fall into place.

2. You are not your last solo.   —*Andrew Rathbun*

Learn the instrument and its role in organized music before trying to anticipate and question the politics and social aspects of the music business—both require personal experience.—*Chuck Rainey*

From Jon Hendricks: Listen.—*Janis Siegel*

Employ ruthless self-criticism in your playing.
—*Jim Babor*

Whatever you're working on or creating, always expand your approach and thinking.
—*Tom Ranier*

This business of music is not a "sprint," but a "long-distance race," **and** the definition of a "successful musician" is a person who plays good music with good people.—*Steve Fidyk*

Don't be late, speak when spoken to, and be a problem solver.—*Dan Carlin*

"It all starts with one good note," a quote from Freddie Gruber. Freddie was getting me to gently drop the sticks onto the kit—right hand on the ride, left hand on the snare—have the bass drum pedal come off the head, and splash the hi-hats, all in perfect unison with a balance that emphasized the bottom. One note! Once I had one good note, then I could advance to two good notes.—*Steve Smith*

 **Let the music tell you what or what not to play.**—*Ed Soph*

From Miles: Finish before you're done! Meaning, if you are going to play something just to fill space, let the rhythm section do it for you, which "might" lead to something more interesting, interactively speaking.—*David Liebman*

Be flexible and easy to work with, with a smile.—*Matt Howard*

Most of your musical life will not be about being a virtuoso— it will be more about trying to contribute just what the moment needs. This also helps you get rehired.—*Larry Koonse*

I had the great honor to study for a few years and become friends with Tony Williams. He told me to "Create a clear and direct line of communication with the listener out in the audience and the members of the band." He said, "They should never misunderstand what you are saying."
—*Gregg Bissonette*

Listen. —*Nathan East*

Buy a metronome.—*Perry Dreiman*

Don't try to imitate others. Learn from them.—*Scott Goodman*

Show up to the rehearsal sounding as if you're ready for the gig. The rehearsal is not the time to learn the material; it is the time to fine-tune the performance. Do the homework!—*Damian Erskine*

Don't rely on the first couple of numbers on the bandstand to warm up—hit the stage at full speed, ready to perform at your top level.—*David Arnay*

When you move through unfamiliar territory (like major record labels populated with tough guys), work on your posture. Carry yourself straight, like you own the joint.—*Jeff Levenson*

"Take care of the music, and the music will take care of you." Heard from Lester Bowie as a young musician in St. Louis, when the Maestro was holding court. It has been truer than not.—*Marty Ehrlich*

 Be yourself; everyone else is taken.—*Russ Ferrante*

It's not who you know that counts, it's who knows you.—*Bob Becker*

"Don't let the gate keepers hold you back."
—*Wayne Shorter to Joe Lovano*

Pay heed to the soft, small voice inside that is trying to tell you what matters. This voice is not loud, but it will not go away easily. If you listen to it, wonderful things are possible. I paraphrase this advice from Abraham Maslow's *Towards a Psychology of Being.*—*Marc Copland*

Dreams Don'T work unLess You Do. You create Your own good Luck.
—*Matt Wilson*

> Practice, practice,
> practice, practice, practice,
> practice, practice,
> and never give up.—*Kenny Aronoff*

Less is more. Every composer prefers to have a tighter lyric, which gives them the room to write a more expressive melody. Every vocalist prefers a tighter lyric, which allows them the space to give greater expression in their vocals.
—*Marty Panzer*

Hear, think, and play in long phrases.
—*Marcio Doctor*

Be a nice person, and try to get along with everyone.—*Luis Conte*

Don't be late for the job.—*John Beck*

You can't win if you don't play.—*George S. Clinton*

👍 Don't compare yourself to your icons. They came up in a totally different musical and business climate.
—*John Beasley*

Read or play something new in music every day!—*Emil Richards*

Don't be afraid to make mistakes! You will learn far more from the mistakes you make than all of your successes.—*Bob Barry*

If you want to play bad enough you will play! You have to seriously want it.—*Joe LaBarbera*

The eraser is the most important part of the pencil.
—*Bruce Broughton*

Space is as important as the notes.—*Ralph Humphrey*

Never play in apnea; Always breathe freely when playing, and be aware of it.—*Cecilia Tsan*

From one of the Basie band saxophonists: "Play pretty," which I interpreted to mean make a nice sound with your instrument. Too often students of jazz neglect dynamics, timbral possibilities, and playing a compelling melody on the quest to playing good notes.
—*Bob Mintzer*

"When you can't come up with anything original, it's okay to imitate yourself."
—*Shelly Manne to Ruth Price*

Pay attention to your teachers and band leaders.—*Ignacio Berroa*

Play what you'd like to hear.—*Jake Reed*

Practice, learn, and study as much as you can now while you're young before "real life" starts to take priority (e.g., bills, a home, family, job, health insurance, etc.).—*Alexa Tarantino*

Listen more, speak less, and always say thank you.
—*Carl Allen*

The manager, and my good friend, Richard Kee from the Pasadena Gym, told me when I had just turned 15: "Whatever you end up doing with your life, don't ever stop training. It will help you with your strength, your reflexes, and your overall awareness. It will mean a lot more to you as you age." He was right, of course.—*Jim Keltner*

At a seminar back in 1972, jazz guitarist Barney Kessel said, "To be a better musician, one should have a well-rounded life. While music is very important, it shouldn't be the only thing that your life is made of." This is fantastic advice!—Grant Geissman

"Music is a drop in the ocean of life."
—Wayne Shorter to Terri Lyne Carrington

Play with conviction, and always try to play with musicians that are above your level. They will raise your game! (Just for fun, Joe Guercio used to say, "If you can't handle the gig, don't take the call.")—*Tim Weston*

The music is the most important, not your technique!—*Joe Pereira*

Keep listening and learning.—*Rick Drumm*

From my dad: Be on time, don't drink on the gig, and always carry an extension cord and a roll of duct tape with you, because with those two items you can handle almost any situation.— *Robin Meloy Goldsby*
(Note: Robin's father was the drummer for Mister Rogers' Neighborhood)

A good way to battle ego issues is to think in this way: it's not about proving your musical worth. It's about what you can uniquely offer to the music in this moment.—*Cuong Vu*

Never burn a bridge. If you are upset to the point of calling it quits or telling someone off, stop and take a time out. Decisions made in moments of extreme emotion are often not the best ones.
—*Liesl Whitaker*

Best advice came from my mother when I was 10 years old: "Michael, put away your baseball glove for good, and practice the vibraphone."—Mike Mainieri

Keep writing, learn the best of other people's songs—the ones that move you—learn from musical traditions, and eventually you'll have enough good songs of your own to perform. Oh, and don't judge your success by how many recordings you sell.—*Anne Hills*

 Shut up and listen.—*Christian McBride*

Billy Hart told me the word "jazz" was a sociological development demonstrated through music.—*Ethan Iverson*

As a young musician it was "be the last one in and the first one out [Bud Herseth, legendary principal trumpet of the Chicago Symphony Orchestra]." As a mature musician it was "don't be afraid to take charge, but be ready to pass the baton [Bud Herseth]."—*Ed Carroll*

"Keep your horn on your face!"—George Garzone. He was right. As long as I kept picking up my horn, going to the piano, or consistently showing up for sessions, gigs, rehearsals, and more, everything that seemed to be in my way instantly became a little smaller and easier to deal with.—*Ingrid Jensen*

Always serve the music.—*Otmaro Ruíz*

The best advice from my dad was "follow your heart, and the money will follow."—*Rachel Z. Hakim*

When you feel lost, confused, depressed, or at sea, just do the "next thing." Even if it's taking out the trash. Or taking a bath. Or walking the dog. Or taking a deep breath. Just do the next thing.—*Mary Chapin Carpenter*

Learn your craft!—*Bernard "Pretty" Purdie*

Try not to compare; be inspired instead.
—*Anne Hills*

Play to make others sound good. Playing music in a band is about the collective.—*John Beasley*

Don't try to be what you think others expect you to be. Somewhere inside, you know what you want to be and what you want to do. —*Shelly Berg*

Leave space. —*John Scofield*

The great Ron Carter once said, "There are three registers on the bass: the upper register, the middle register, and the cash register.

—*Benjamin Williams*

Believe in yourself. Be *your* best, not someone else's. —*Vinnie Colaiuta*

From my "guitar guru" Pepe Romero: "Fill every moment you spend with your instrument with deep gratitude for the blessings of music-making." —*William Kanengiser*

Along with striving to be a good musician, be a good colleague; always strive to be a decent human being. —*Lynn Helding*

One thing that has always stayed with me was some advice my father gave me. He said, "Hire good people, and let them do their job. They are the experts in their field." —*Tim Ishii*

My favorite teacher, Kenton Terry, told me [something] which made the biggest difference in my playing: "You dress with style. Why don't you play with style?" —*Judith Johanson*

The best advice I have ever received was being taught to show respect to those who have "been there and done that"—those who have come before me and proved themselves both personally and musically. Doing this has always elicited respect in return. We should never forget that we stand on the shoulders of all those who have come before us.

—*Marvin Stamm*

When you
play music,
pay more attention
to others than
yourself. In your life,
think big.
—*Bill Cunliffe*

**Don't listen
so hard; do
your job.**
—*John Riley*

Shake music's hand, and wait for a response.
—*Curt Moore*

Re: writing—keep your publishing, and trust that the personal is universal (re: lyrics). Re: studio and the band—be early, clean up your charts, and organize the book.—*Shelby Flint*

**Show up to the gig before
the bandleader gets there.
If you're the bandleader,
get there first.**—*Brian Andres*

**Be versatile—strive to put a
multilayered career together.**—*Steve Houghton*

Don't compare yourself
or your life to others.
—*Kenny Werner*

**It came from David Bowie, when he said as he
laughed, "Maria, it's just music! If the plane goes
down, everyone walks away!"**—*Maria Schneider*

Wisdom from a Studio Legend

Here are some of my father's (Tommy Tedesco) sage bits of advice for the student—coming from a guitar player's perspective, but it works in every field. I've used a few in my world, and I don't play an instrument.

1. Listen to all kinds of guitar players. Know their names and the style they are known for. This helps when a leader asks for a specific style of guitar playing.

2. When you are taking a break from practicing and are relaxing watching TV, play your guitar softly. Work on techniques. Your eyes and ears will be watching TV, but your hands will be busy building technique in your off time.

3. When you take a job, it should have one or more of these qualities:
   a. Good money
   b. Fun
   c. Connections for the future
   d. Learning

   If it doesn't have any of these, forget it. Move on.

4. When someone helps you in your career, make a special call to thank him or her. It's the least you can do for the effort.

5. Sit in with strange groups when you get a chance. It provides more outlets to getting future work.

6. Learn from each other. I have picked up things from other guitar players that were movers. Don't be jealous of each other. Share your experiences and licks, and you will both be farther ahead.

7. Try to go to an occasional pop concert even though you might not like the music. Spend time watching the conductor. This will end up being an extremely valuable experience.

8. Never lose it on the leader even if you're 110 percent right. Weigh the consequences. Assume you won't get another job from that person, and be prepared.

9. When you get to work and you find the donuts, bite into three of them. Eat one. You can guarantee when you come back throughout the day, the other two will be left there.

   —*Denny Tedesco (Son of legendary studio guitarist Tommy Tedesco of Wrecking Crew fame)*

And, this timeless quote from Papa Jo Jones:

> "Always start basic, and you'll never go wrong... after you have control of your instrument, you can do whatever you wish. Regardless of whatever they name it: **you play.**"

The Best Advice I've Ever Given

Play what *you* like, not what you think you should be playing or what other people tell you to play. Develop your own individual style.—*Janet Paulus*

Try to play your story! And don't forget that music, first of all, is sound!—*Rita Marcotulli*

Have a positive attitude.
—*Catina DeLuna*

Work hard and accept everything that is given to you in life.—*George Garzone*

Live in gratitude, humility, integrity, with no expectation.—*John Daversa*

Always use your "ears" to produce the sound you wish to express.—*Don Shelton*

Be true and honest—to yourself and the music.—*Matt Harris*

 Be patient with others; you don't know what they are going through.
—*Gary Burton*

No matter what you plan to do with music, get as comfortable as you can with playing the piano.
—*Jennifer Barnes*

Be professional. As much fun as participating in music is, it is a **profession**!—*Leland Sklar*

Keep evolving and always have big ears.
—*Glenn Kotche*

Probably passing along my father's advice to me: don't be cheap. Pay the band as well as you can, and don't be afraid to ask for a good fee.
—*Tierney Sutton*

When talking to young composers, I usually advise them to take every possible opportunity. You never know who you're going to meet and where a project is going to take you.
—*David Schwartz*

LISTEN TO THE GROUP AS IF YOU WERE IN THE AUDIENCE, AND PLAY WHAT YOU WANT TO HEAR, NOT AS PLAYER, BUT AS A MUSIC LOVER.
—*Damian Erskine*

The development of an artist never stops—and that's a great and profound blessing.—*Tom Ranier*

Believe in yourself. Be open and ready for opportunity—it can come in a disguise. Learn your craft thoroughly. Allow and welcome mistakes. Be kind, especially to yourself.—*Janis Siegel*

 # Put in the time.—*Steve Smith*

Breathe.—*Alan Pasqua*

As an improviser, be in the present—there's no tomorrow or yesterday; nor is there the conditional tense (would've, should've, etc.)...it's too late for that...only the present.
—*David Liebman*

Work hard, be nice, and get lucky.—*Dan Carlin*

Don't underestimate the power of fundamentals and technique. Also, learn to play with a metronome properly.
—*Matt Howard*

Be open to learning from musical genres that aren't your first choice. There [are] all kinds of information that will serve you well and inform your musical choices outside of your chosen path.
—*Larry Koonse*

Don't be afraid to admit you're wrong or that you made a mistake. Learn from it. Great ideas are born from mistakes.—*John DeChristopher*

Buy a metronome.—*Perry Dreiman*

It's inhumane to measure yourself according to someone else's/society's definition of "success" or "failure." Likewise, it's inhumane to measure others according to your definition of "success" or "failure."—*Michelle Makarski*

Have fun. Don't beat yourself over the head.—*Scott Goodman*

Just be yourself! —*Satnam Ramgotra*

[I ask] my students to try to sing a phrase first and then try to play it the same way on their instruments. We have to sing with our instruments.—*Pamela Havenith*

Stop beating yourself up by trying to be somebody else. —*David Arnay*

👍 **Listen! God gave you two ears and one mouth. Use proportionally.**—*Jeff Levenson*

Always, at the first rehearsal, ask the leader if she/he/they have lost weight.—*Marty Ehrlich*

There's no one as wrong as the one who knows all the answers.—*Russ Ferrante*

Listen!—*Skip Hadden*

👍 **Make dust or eat dust.**—*Bob Becker*

Live in the Library of the Sounds & Spirits of the Masters. —*Joe Lovano*

Play music that you can feel and hear.
Listen first, play second.—*Marc Copland*

If you can sing it, you can play it.—*Marcio Doctor*

Do not love playing your instrument more than playing the song.—*Matt Wilson*

Create a plan that you execute to reach your goal.
Practice! There are no shortcuts to success!—*Kenny Aronoff*

Creativity is an act of rebellion. You have to break some rules to create something new.—*Claus Hessler*

Don't be late for the job.—*John Beck*
Serve the situation.—*Adam Nussbaum*

I repeat what Miles told me, "Get your own band." Find your voice and stick to it, whether its media composer, instrumentalist, singer, or songwriter.—*John Beasley*

Play from the heart.—*Su-a Lee*

Listen, listen, and listen some more.—*Joe LaBarbera*

Never fall into the trap of competing with others in your field. You have only one competitor, and that's you! Am I better today than I was yesterday?—*Bob Barry*

Composing is like playing an instrument: it takes lots of practice to get proficient.—*Bruce Broughton*

Follow your heart.—*John Clayton*

You don't get to sing a song until you thoroughly and honestly understand the lyric.—*Ruth Price*

With shoulders down, use natural gravity to produce the sound rather than force. I realized that it can apply to almost any instrument. The quality of the tone is immediately enhanced.—*Cecilia Tsan*

Make a nice sound. Learn how to play a melody. Work on time, melody, and harmony. Play the piano and drums. Show up early and be on the team. Project gratitude and positivity in everything you do. Check out all kinds of music. Be a composer/arranger/instigator. Try to formulate a musical philosophy and frame it in composition. Develop a posse of like-minded musicians. Eat well, exercise, and get enough rest. Think well.—*Bob Mintzer*

**Good music tells you what to play.
Not so good music may not and makes
your job harder and less fun.**—*Ralph Humphrey*

Don't let any situation or anyone interfere with your dreams.
—*Ignacio Berroa*

Record yourself.—*Jake Reed*

**Music is a lifelong quest. Never assume
that you have figured it all out.**—*Gary Hobbs*

Make sure to schedule time into your calendar
just for yourself. It is important to have time
to recharge so that when you are performing or
teaching, you can give those experiences
the energy and commitment that they deserve.
—*Alexa Tarantino*

**Play your best on every single gig. It doesn't matter
if it is a $30 gig or a $500 gig—you never know who
is listening, watching.**—*Rosa Avila*

*Don't be afraid of hearing no, and find out what
your gift is, and make it your life's mission to
make it happen.*—*Carl Allen*

**Don't let your gift die. Being young and careless is generally
the path most of us take. So being aware, early on, of the
pitfalls should make a difference in your later years. Kind of
preachy but very important!**—*Jim Keltner*

Never stop playing after a mistake; power
through and push forward. No one will
even notice, and you'll be the better for it.
Some truly great riffs have happened
via the mistake!—*Danny Seraphine*

**Don't be afraid to play in your own voice,
no matter what the current trend is.**—*Grant Geissman*

Invest in your own career. Spend your own money (if/when you can) on your artistic endeavors, and take responsibility for your destiny as best you can. Feels better when you succeed. And not easy to blame others.—*Terri Lyne Carrington*

👍**Always remain curious.**—*Joe Pereira*

Present your (printed) music to others, your bandmates, as you would want to see it yourself! Don't be sloppy and lazy!—*Steve Khan*

The fear of making a mistake has already played out a thousand times in your head. It's already happened. It can't get worse. So just go play, now!—*Liesl Whitaker*

Shut up and listen.—*Christian McBride*

Honesty is everything.—*Tim Weston*

Be ready to grow in unexpected ways. No career, for a sensitive musician, is linear.—*Ed Carroll*

Be open and present, and don't hang on to your mistakes while you're performing; note them for later. Learn to take a compliment without pointing out your mistakes, because that's dismissing of someone else's experience. Be gracious and thankful, if you get to do what you love.—*Anne Hills*

Do something. Take a step. You can always change direction, but standing still gets you nowhere.—*Tim Ishii*

When putting together a band for a gig, my first thought (from when I was a teenage bandleader) was, "Who should I call to play drums?" I can deal with a bass player that is a little bit of a thumper...I'd just bring charts [and] at least he'd play the correct roots...BUT, a drummer with bad time and/or [who] couldn't swing, for me, is an absolute nightmare.—*Mike Mainieri*

As a songwriter, I believe in writing down ideas, thoughts, emotions, and feelings as they occur... the raw material, if you will, of song ideas. (If you're in the car, record them on your phone.) I cannot be certain I will remember them later, so I always carry a little Moleskine book and a pen...it's with me in my backpack wherever I go. The tools of my trade.

—*Mary Chapin Carpenter*

Treat your improvisations as if you are composing, especially in ballads. Make each solo relatable to the original song (avoid the "one solo fits all" approach).—Otmaro Ruíz

Always know where **1** is, and it's about dynamics, feel, and counting.

—*Bernard "Pretty" Purdie*

I would advise any musician, young or old, to be a "team player." It will be much appreciated by your peers and colleagues more than you realize and will make them want to work and make music with you.—*Marvin Stamm*

I tell my students who have problems with nerves: take a deep breath, and remember you are playing for them (the listening public)!—*Judith Johanson*

Leave space—we all try to learn how to fill it up, but it's essential to leave space. Breathe and make room for the other musicians—never just listen to yourself, listen to who you're playing with and fit in. When we practice at home we're alone so we have to constantly remind ourselves to listen and leave space when we play with people. The soloist has to fit in with the band just as much as the "accompanists" have to fit in with the soloist. It's a **band!**—*John Scofield*

Finding the one note that your audience will never forget is infinitely better than anything your virtuosity might display. You can't make that happen, but you do have to trust that it will happen.—*Shelly Berg*

Follow your passion, even if it doesn't make sense to others. —*Gary Motley*

> Learn a piece by first practicing it slowly with a metronome and then gradually increasing the tempo. —*Raynor Carroll*

Be yourself. You're all you've got. —*Vinnie Colaiuta*

The problem isn't with your hands and feet; it's a lack of clarity in your ideas and your brain not sending the signals to your limbs early enough so that the hands and feet can execute your ideas in a relaxed, flowing way. Practicing slowly yields a deeper understanding and quicker progress. —*John Riley*

I have two, for singers who breathe for a living:

1. Every time you breathe, you create your instrument anew. The truth of this should blow your mind. When an instrumentalist takes their hands away from their instrument, even for a moment, when they return, they can expect to find the same instrument they left a few seconds before. Not so for singers: because our instrument is the vocal tract, our instrument is infinitely changeable and resets every time we breathe.

2. The quality of the air next to your face is the same as the air across the room. Don't travel across the room to get the air.

—*Lynn Helding*

Be the kind of person other musicians like to be around. All else will likely follow. —*Curt Moore*

Life isn't a straight line. It is a patchwork quilt. Don't be disheartened by events that don't fit the path you expected for yourself. Everything that happens to you (and how you deal with it) is a part of who you are. Treasure it. —*Kristin Korb*

Talent gets you so far. Hard work can take you all the way.—*Neil Percy*

There's already been a Jaco. Play like you.
—*Jeff Dalton*

Make friends with the stagehands and the sound guys.—*Bob Breithaupt*

My favorite advice to myself is: treasure what you cannot do.—*Makoto Ozone*

Never, ever date the boss. Stick to the rhythm section.
—*Robin Meloy Goldsby*

Play as if you're singing.—*Christine Pendrill*

I'm not sure, because I'm not on the receiving end. But I tell others and myself that when they are making music, to try and always stay connected with the joy and excitement from when you first made music—when it was only about music, and not about being scrutinized.
—*Maria Schneider*

 Try to follow your inspiration, not your fears.—*Kenny Werner*

SECTION 11
IN THEIR OWN WORDS... MORE ADVICE FROM THE PROS

In the interest of readability, we decided to include a good number of quotes within the main body of our text, but the following advice merits inclusion and your attention.

More Sight-Reading Advice

Practice sight-reading! Learn how to prepare, and look at what's coming.—*Janet Paulus*

Sight-read every day, starting in a slow, steady tempo. Keep going even if you make a mistake.—Catina DeLuna

Don't rush!—*Charlie Bisharat*

1. Learn theory and harmony as deeply as you can, which will help you recognize key centers, shapes, and relationships instead of just one note to the next. **2.** What's past is past—forget about it, and keep looking to what's coming up! (You can assess and improve later, but you need all your focus on the present moment!)—*Jennifer Barnes*

Make sight-reading a part of your daily practice routine. As a complement to sight-reading, learn a non-Western [style of] music that is taught by rote.—*Russell Hartenberger*

Be brave! If you're not, pretend to be. And, look ahead.—*Ellen Seeling*

Read down as well as across.—*Skip Hadden*

Learning to Look Ahead is critical to good sight-reading.—*Don Shelton*

Read something every day.—*Andrew Rathbun*

There's no way around it, you just have to do it a bunch.—*Matt Howard*

Start slowly. Don't try to go fast at first. Look for common shapes and rhythms (i.e., triads, scales, familiar harmony).—*Matt Harris*

Own and practice from the Louis Bellson
Modern Reading in $\frac{4}{4}$ **book.**—*Tim Kobza*

Before you sight-read the chart, take a pencil (or I prefer to commit with a Sharpie), and put double bar lines after 4-, 8-, or 16-bar phrases...most sight-reading train wrecks occur when the musician gets lost or doesn't feel an odd-bar phrase. Also, circle or highlight repeat signs, 1st and 2nd endings, D.S. and Coda signs, and tempo changes.—*Gregg Bissonette*

See the big picture. If you miss something, keep the train rolling by being ready with the next thing.—*David Arnay*

Learn as much music as you can internally. Learn to hear and feel it. Use charts as guides, not as the law.—*Marc Copland*

Check out the intro and the ending and, most importantly, offer a clear and comfortable time melody so your fellow musicians can welcome their parts with ease.—*Matt Wilson*

Go from a macro to a micro perspective: acknowledge first the overall structure, then identify the inner sections and then the details.
—*Marcio Doctor*

Check the intro and the ending; everything else will be OK.—*Joe LaBarbera*

Read everything you can get your hands on.—*Bruce Broughton*

Get the road map first; get the rest if you can.
Don't be afraid to ask up front, what's the feel?—*Jim Payne*

There's no shortcut or natural talent in becoming an excellent sight-reader. You have to pay your dues like all aspiring musicians.—*Joe Porcaro*

Just start doing it; the more you do it, the less afraid you will be.—*Rosa Avila*

Just like any practice regimen, regularity is key. Practice sight-reading 15 minutes a day, and, once you begin a piece, DON'T STOP.—*Allison Miller*

Practice reading a lot of different kinds of material at home to sharpen your skills.—*Grant Geissman*

Learn to look ahead when you have the chance (long note value or rest). Recognize two-beat patterns (different subdivisions), and be able to divide the measure in half. Practice sight-reading.—*Tim Ishii*

I think it's important to familiarize yourself with the many different ways in which charts are written. Then, when you're looking ahead, you'll feel more comfortable having seen those configurations before, giving rise to the confidence so crucially needed in that situation.—*Jim Keltner*

In your private practice time, set the tempo, a metronome, where it is comfortable for YOU—try to practice reading so that you get the feeling that you are doing well at it. Don't set yourself up to fail or to be disappointed.—*Steve Khan*

Learn to sing rhythms like a horn player. Study Sarah Vaughan's scat singing, and memorize her phrasing and vocal sound.—*Danny Gottlieb*

Do it as often as you can, and try to incorporate it in your practice routine whenever possible.—*Benjamin Williams*

For singers, learn bass and treble clefs. Time is tricky for me, so drilling on different patterns would help. No way around lots of practicing. Intervals can be learned through familiar tunes (e.g., the first interval of "Blue Skies" is a fifth).—*Shelby Flint*

Find music that is challenging but not too easy and not too difficult. Read regularly and as often as possible.—*Raynor Carroll*

Look for the "major" information, and approach fills like you're playing with one hand. Others will appreciate the simplicity.—*Bob Breithaupt*

Articulation of phrase—in classical music and big band music, we are required to read and play phrases without mistake, but in other formats (such as small group), I play by my own understanding and as if I am singing. Pay attention to accents and dynamics.—*Sadao Watanabe*

Can you hear the piece before you play it? I love playing violin, flute, oboe, etc., and duets on keyboard instruments with my students. Always play a duet with someone who reads *better* than you! This is both frustrating and fun(!).—*John Tafoya*

Learn to scan at an early age. Like anything else, it takes practice.—*Robin Meloy Goldsby*

During a lesson with Billy Cobham, I asked for his advice on being a better sight-reader. He said: "You live in New York City. You are surrounded by music everywhere you go. Visualize everything you hear in notated form. It doesn't matter if you're walking down the street and hear five seconds of music coming out of a bodega, sitting in a taxi cab with the radio playing, or a boom box blasting as it passes you on the street. You will hear music everywhere. Once you begin to visualize what you are hearing as written music, you will begin to instantly recognize those phrases when you see them written on a chart in front of you."—*Doane Perry*

If I receive the music in advance, I go to a copy shop and have it enlarged. Advice to composers using Sibelius or other similar writing programs: if you compose a tune in A♭, don't let the program determine the placement of sharps or flats (i.e. A♭ scale ≠ G♯ A♯ B♯ C♯ D♯ E♯ G G♯). Take the time: go through the score and correct those "errors."

—*Mike Mainieri*

More Business Advice

Be smart with money; invest and buy a good instrument as soon as you know this is the life you want.—*Aaron Serfaty*

Just go for it full out, or have an alternative future in place.—*Ruth Price*

Respect and Appreciate every single person who works for you: musicians, stage staff, promoters, audience, and more.—*Makoto Ozone*

Never be afraid to Ask for What You Need—monetarily speaking—within reason.—*Don Shelton*

Learn what it takes early on to get your music out there in front of people, but do this in a natural, organic way. Be genuine and realistic. Don't be overly aggressive and push only your own agenda.—*Andrew Rathbun*

It's hard to balance finance and art. After a while, you get a sense of what you're truly worth, and you should ask for it. On the other hand, I think there are many situations where it's great to donate your musical services to charities, friends, etc.—*David Schwartz*

Receive payment before or directly after your performance.—*Joe Corsello*

Be open to sharing the knowledge and teaching. Not only is it gratifying to pass down information to younger generations, but it can create a steady paycheck in lean times.—*Larry Koonse*

For string players, buying and insuring instruments, especially by famous makers, can sometimes bankrupt you, especially during the early part of your career. There are presently some new violin makers who will present you with authentic certificates to go with wonderful instruments, a few of which can even compete with some of the old masters.—*Pamela Havenith*

The people on the business side—promoters, record company folks, etc.—are for the most part in this for one reason. They are fascinated by the music and by you, the artist. Try to connect with them, and be who you really are. That said, be able to switch gears at the drop of a hat—be aware and able to protect yourself. It's a labor of love, but it's also your livelihood.—*Marc Copland*

Do something every day in order to realize your goal as a musician.—*Kenny Aronoff*

Try to learn something new from every music job that you are given to play!—*Emil Richards*

When negotiating a fee, have in your mind what you think would be twice too much, what would be a generous fee, what they will probably offer, and what you are willing to settle for. Don't accept unless you would do it without pay anyway.—*Abbie Conant*

Compose, compose, compose...publish it all. For vibraphonists, be a bandleader!—*Mike Mainieri*

Have an agent and a good music lawyer...learn the business to control your success.—*Bernard "Pretty" Purdie*

Become financially independent. Get your finances together by educating yourself, setting and sticking to budgets, and avoiding credit cards and loans.—*Raynor Carroll*

Don't confuse music with the music business.—*Gary Motley*

Unfortunately, the music is not enough. Marketing yourself may not be of equal importance to your musical skill set, but it's right up there. Master your musical goals while also gaining the tools to present yourself to the world so that opportunities open themselves up to you. There is no one path to accomplish this. Find yours.—*Gordon Goodwin*

If you're in a union or performance organization (SAG, AFTRA, BMI, ASCAP, etc.), be aware of what support the organization may offer, and seek good contacts/ relationships there.— *Shelby Flint*

The trend in my lifetime is that big corporate interests keep trying to find ways of taking income from artists, and they continually succeed. Becoming a very versatile musician with a wide range of tastes is the best way to insure your survival. Be sure to follow through on the opportunities that come your way.—*Chris Brubeck*

Be organized. Be professional.
Live within your means.—*Brian Andres*

Plan your career as a music professional—imagine what skills you'll need to sustain you until you are in your sixties or seventies.—*Bob Breithaupt*

Save your money, take lessons with the best possible teachers, and learn to make a promo package. If you're a leader, lead with grace and compassion, for you were once in your sideman's shoes. This allows you to lead with confidence and humility, and the result is respect from your fellow musical companions.—*John L. Worley, Jr.*

There are a ton of great players, but only a few successful ones. What differentiates them from the rest is being on time, and being nice, [being] flexible, and [having] the will to leave their ego behind.
—*Jeff Dalton*

Look for venues that are friendly to your style. Develop a personal narrative with the booking contact, and always follow up. Be persistent in a respectful way. Sell yourself by highlighting what makes "you" different and unique.
—*Paul Vornhagen*

Always say "yes" to any performance opportunity, and always show up early with a smile on your face (even if you've had a terrible day!). Be professional—know your music entirely. Don't be that musician that "counts and plays."—*John Tafoya*

Don't forget that you are building relationships, whether it is with bookers, the press, fans, or your fellow musicians.—Kristin Korb

Stay visible when you're starting your career or starting anew in a different place—show up to hear others share their artistry, and make the effort to meet people at concerts and other musical gatherings.—Joanne Pearce Martin

If you are lucky enough to ever be in a position to pay others for their work, be honest and be fair. Fairness, fiscal generosity (when deserved), and generosity of spirit will go a long way in creating a good working environment where everyone feels valued.—Doane Perry

Be very, very good at at least one thing. Make sure people know you're the best at that one thing. It's even better if you're very good at three or four things.—John Goldsby

Best Overall Advice I've Ever Received

Stay relevant; changes in music and business are evident.—*Ivan Hampden, Jr.*

1. Picasso: "The good borrow, the great steal." It served him well. Me, too.
2. Be discovered, not found out.
3. Believe in yourself, but never be arrogant or cocky.
4. Never stop asking, searching, or learning.
5. The "KISS" system really works: keep it simple, stupid.—*Jiggs Whigham*

Everyone has a story to tell. Never give up, put everything you have into your artistic dream. If you don't you will never know if it would have come true!—*Bart Marantz*

First, a brief disclaimer. As a woman trumpet player with a 45-year professional career, I believe my experience has been very different from that of my male colleagues. And so I want to speak here to women and girls who are contemplating a career in jazz, or young women players who are just starting out. "Don't let the haters get you down." Plan on getting a lot of rejection, and be prepared. Blow it off, and don't quit. Persistence pays!—*Ellen Seeling*

Always play or sing with the best Musicality you can and with Expression.—*Don Shelton*

Be honest, be a good person, and be yourself. The people who influenced me most in my life and in my career were my dad, Armand Zildjian, Vic Firth, and Lennie DiMuzio. And, they all gave me that advice without ever actually saying it.
—*John DeChristopher*

"Always remain humble!" Casey Scheuerell is the culprit of that advice to me, and I think about it daily to this day!—*Satnam Ramgotra*

The only way to become a master musician is to pass it on.—*Allison Miller*

Musically: No matter what instrument you play, study Debussy's Sonata for Flute, Viola, and Harp. Professionally: Always meet your deadlines, and always be on time; that will justify your being able to demand the same of others.—*Jeff Ernstoff*

ADVICE #1: Henry Mancini told me, "Kid, don't be an arranger, be a composer—that's where the money is!" When I got to that fork in the road, I took his advice, became a busy TV composer, and am still benefitting from those earnings. However, as an artist, I have never stopped arranging, as it has given me much musical and personal gratification over the years.

ADVICE #2: While studying with my mentor, arranger Billy Byers, he remarked, "There are a number of formulas for writing charts." When I asked him what they were, he refused to tell me, because he didn't want to give me shortcuts, and I would have to find my own way of doing things. That has served me well, as I was forced to "reinvent the wheel" and find a unique approach every time I picked up the pencil.—*Nan Schwartz*

I was advised to change trumpet instructors after a bad experience with an artist teacher during my high school years. His "education through intimidation approach" made me doubt my ability to succeed, and I quit trumpet for a couple months. My high school band director referred me to a teacher who had just graduated from college. His name is Joe Clouse, and he helped me address areas in need of improvement while still making me feel good about what I had learned so far.—Jeff Jarvis

Oddly, "Don't give so much." My then teacher, the amazing Branimir
  Slokar, said this when I was preparing a concerto that I was to play with
an orchestra in a few weeks. He could have said, "Don't try so hard," but
  I wouldn't have understood that. I was trying to give everything when I
played, and in a sense, I was, but I was exhausting myself and stressing
  myself out. Somehow, his words helped me understand that I just needed
to play from the center of my being, from my heart, and that was more
  than enough. So simple.—*Abbie Conant*

The late great Phil Ramone pulled me aside after I had berated a second
engineer at the Record Plant for accidentally clipping (erasing part of) my
original drum track while I was overdubbing fills on it. He reminded me
that these are people, not machines, and they make mistakes, especially
working late into the wee hours of the morning trying to make our record
perfect. Always strive to make the people around you better and support
them. They will go to the wall for you, and you'll be the better man for it.
—*Danny Seraphine*

If someone tells you there's only one way to hold a stick, run the other way.—*Jim Chapin to Claus Hessler*

**Every note that's played is important, so make every
note count...and, yes, this advice came from Peter. It made
me a solid musician and changed my life.**—*Rosa Avila*

*Always play at your top level as you never know who could be listening;
play with your subconscious mind as though you are listening to
a finished recording, allowing your body to respond to the music;
finish college; put as much money into a retirement account as
possible from every paycheck; exercise as much as possible; arrive
early for your gigs; do as much homework, study, and preparation
before each engagement as you can. Respect the leader or conductor,
and never embarrass him or her.*—*Danny Gottlieb*

Work hard and play hard. Take chances. Being prepared for a performance
gives you the freedom to take liberties onstage and really connect with
the people around you.—*Alyssa Park*

"Never feel too settled"—I took this to mean always be searching for ways to improve your playing/musicianship skills, and always be looking for the next opportunity, another job that will challenge you and make you a better player.—*John Tafoya*

Embrace your own sound.—*Gary Motley*

Be flexible. Present the music as you see fit, but be able to adapt to the conductor, ensemble, venue, etc.—*Raynor Carroll*

Ralph Peña advised me to develop chromatic or stepwise phrases/lines rather than jump all over the bass!—*Chuck Berghofer*

ALWAYS PLAY EVERY GIG AS IF IT WAS CARNEGIE HALL IN TERMS OF YOUR EFFORT AND THE QUALITY YOU ASPIRE TO. I HAVE LEARNED AFTER MANY DECADES OF PERFORMING THAT YEARS DOWN THE ROAD SOMEONE YOU IMPRESSED IN A SMALL AUDIENCE 30 YEARS BEFORE CAN GO ON TO BECOME A BIG DEAL IN THE FIELD AND HIRE YOU TO BE INVOLVED IN A VERY MEANINGFUL PROJECT. (THIS IS ADVICE I HAVE GIVEN TO MYSELF HAVING LIVED IT.)—*Chris Brubeck*

Always allow yourself time for something unexpected to happen on the way to a gig.—*Bob Breithaupt*

Play half the notes you want to play; say half the words that are in your head.—*Jeff Dalton*

Practice! Suggested by every musician I admire and have been lucky enough to get to know and work with. It's the common denominator for all great artists, so there must be something to it?—*Neil Percy*

Ray Brown told me to "turn the wheel" when playing songs in other keys. At the time, I was young and clueless about the cycle and how it could be used. It was truly a life-changing moment for me.—*Kristin Korb*

In the upper left-hand corner of the music part you are handed, never forget that *it does not say* "Steve Khan"—it just says "guitar," which means that any competent guitarist can play this part—*you* are not that special!—*Steve Khan*

"Bring who you are to the music." Billy Higgins told me this in a lesson in 1992.—*Aaron Serfaty*

Best advice I ever got was from Steve Swallow: if you think you might want a life as a musician, forget about it...too many dues, too much frustration and heartache, too little reward. But if you really need to be a musician, the way you need to breathe, then it's the most richly rewarding and soul-satisfying life you could ever possibly hope for.—*Fred Simon*

I was lucky enough to study with the inventively eccentric and unique Barry Altschul. He would have me sing a phrase and then immediately try to play it. He wanted me to be able to instantly orchestrate any idea I had on the drumset. I realized he was trying to help me make an immediate connection between the brain and the limbs, so there was no delay between conceptualizing an idea and responding to another musician. He said, "If you can hear it, then sing it, and then play it, you are creating a direct connection between your thoughts and their execution."—*Doane Perry*

Work hard to be your best, and always make the music come first.—*Joanne Pearce Martin*

Stay true to yourself.—*Dale Hikawa Silverman*
Teach what you know.—*John Goldsby*

Best Overall Advice I've Ever Given

Know your craft, know your worth, build relationships.—*Ivan Hampden, Jr.*

Never give up. Never stop practicing. Never stop loving it. If I'm not loving it, then I'm not in the moment. To help avoid plateaus in your playing, keep exploring (such as finding new ways of sound production).—*Dale Hikawa Silverman*

Play with intention and conviction. Listen intently.
—*Aaron Serfaty*

I'm not sure if others agree that it's my best advice, but I do like to say, "No practice is ever wasted."—*Joanne Pearce Martin*

a) Never practice the principal's solos, and be first in the tea queue.

b) Make eye contact with the conductor and smile!
—*Christine Pendrill*

Don't stop trying—it's the only guaranteed way to fail.—*Brian Malouf*

Most of us string players come from the classical tradition and as such have had less exposure to music on a "grid." My advice is to spend time recording in a home studio so you can really hear (and see) how your playing lines up rhythmically.—*Charlie Bisharat*

Don't steal someone's time. They can always replace their money, but never their time—if they are coming to hear you perform, reward them with all you have, and present your art at the highest level of performance. ***Always.***—*Bart Marantz*

When it comes to your career, no doesn't mean no. It may mean not yet, or not with those particular people, or not until you get certain skills together; but it never means no until you decide it means no.
—*Antonio García*

The best advice I have ever given is not always advice that I remember giving. From time to time, former students have told me that a certain thing I told them affected their life in a substantial way. Often, I don't remember having said it. The lesson I take from this is to always speak to others with honesty and sincerity.—Russell Hartenberger

Music is a process of progress. Keep working toward your goals in a systematic and organized way, and enjoy the journey.—*Steve Fidyk*

Every rut starts out as a groove.—*George S. Clinton*

To young musicians: Find a way to get out of debt, and save money every month.—*Tim Kobza*

Don't kiss up to try to get gigs (some of them already taken); your talent is good enough.—*Luis Conte*

1. Don't overlook great projects that call upon your overall musicianship that do **not** include performing and/or composing, etc. For example, be able to propose/conceptualize and/or research a musical special event or project, such as being the music researcher for a film about the Gershwins, or choosing musical selections for a fireworks spectacular, or choosing the international music for the ceremonial entrance of the Olympic athletes. These supplementary gigs are out there; keep your eyes and ears open, and get at least **three short-term gigs** with **good** production companies.

2. Learn how to **write** an articulate and concise proposal/description of any project(s) you have in mind. Many great ideas don't come to fruition or get adequate funding because the written description of them is poor.

3. If you have your own group, try to somehow differentiate it from others that are similar.   —*Jeff Ernstoff*

Practice slow to play fast. Actually given to me by Sonny Igoe, but I pass it on.—*Jim Payne*

I tell all my students to look at the past as well as the future.—*Ethan Iverson*

Try to learn something new in music every day!—*Emil Richards*

Find your own voice. The more it sounds like you, the more distinctive it is. Only **you** have your voice. Write about something or with an angle on something that has **not** been written about 1,000 times already. Make every lyric you write the best it can be. It doesn't matter if it takes an hour or a year. You can only succeed with the **best creation**. Everyone only hears the finished product. Always make sure it's the best it can possibly be. It's worth all the time and effort it takes.—*Marty Panzer*

You should try early music.—*Abbie Conant*

I've tried to tell my students over the years to not be too myopic about music. To live a well-rounded life. Go out in nature, enjoy art, and cultivate other interests. To find their bliss!—*John Ramsay*

Copy and absorb as much great music as you can.—*Bill Cunliffe*

"Always play the truth."—I once told this to Glenn Kotche when he studied drumset with me. He later credited it in his **Modern Drummer** cover story (August 2007) with becoming an important concept for him when he was making his recording **Mobile**, as well as for his band Wilco when they were recording **Yankee Hotel Foxtrot**.—*Paul Wertico*

Practice and drill 'til you're confident, then forget about it during performance—trust your preparation, and take some chances.—*Shelby Flint*

Stay curious and open to new opportunities.—*Rick Drumm*

In your desire to "get work," don't lose track of developing your own voice.—*Alan Hall*

I tell my university students to measure their words when working with young musicians. It only takes a few minutes to inspire or deter a student from pursuing music as a career or a vocation. If you don't know the answer to a student's question, tell them you'll find out, rather than trying to save face by fabricating an answer.—*Jeff Jarvis*

Keep your horn on your face!—*Ingrid Jensen*

Study with the best teachers that you can.—*Danny Gottlieb*

It's not about you; it's the message that you transmit to the audience.
—*William Kanengiser*

I guess telling my audiences (clinics) how important reading music (drum parts) really is.—*Hal Blaine*

Never compare yourself to anyone else. You are on your own path. You can be inspired by others, but be true to yourself.—*Alyssa Park*

The same things that make a good person are the same things that make a good bass player: patience, humility, selflessness, confidence, and the desire to contribute to the greater good.
—*Benjamin Williams*

When we improvise, we are spontaneously orchestrating.—*John Goldsby*

I encourage young students to be honest about their strengths and weaknesses, and not to spend time pretending to be something they are not. It's more important to stay humble, open-minded, and hard-working, and your path will unfold.—*Gordon Goodwin*

It's hard to predict what the future of music will be, so **be flexible**—be open to many different ideas and many other styles of music. **Be passionate** about what it is you want to do, and **be ready** and **do your homework**.—*John Tafoya*

I heard and met a fine high school musician; told them they were super talented, pointed the way to a place of higher education where they could get a big scholarship; stayed after them to apply; watched them get the opportunity, grow musically, and later saw them featured in **Downbeat Magazine** *as a major new talent with great reviews.*—*Chris Brubeck*

Be on time. Be prepared. Be nice.—*Brian Andres*

I recall working with a technically excellent but inexperienced young musician who was determined to show everyone what he could do— ridiculously overplaying in the process. Finally, I emphatically implored him to "just relax and leave some air and breathing room in the music for the other musicians!" Miraculously, I think he listened because he began to settle down and ultimately ended up being a pretty good team player.—*Doane Perry*

More Travel Advice

Keep it light.—*Jim Payne*

Watch what you eat, but try to be as accommodating as possible. Also, have breakfast!—*Aaron Serfaty*

Hydrate! (I generally don't have to carry an instrument, so I'm concentrating on health here.)—*Joanne Pearce Martin*

Be kind to people. Be aware of the cultural aspects of your travel.—*Ivan Hampden, Jr.*

Although "you gotta do what you gotta do" to enjoy playing music as well as make a living in music, you will always be making changes through personal experiences—being kind to those who are helping.—*Chuck Rainey*

Make time at the end of a tour to really immerse yourself in the culture.—*Charlie Bisharat*

Be adventurous and try new things, whether food, experiences, music, or anything else!—*Jennifer Barnes*

Always put everything essential (music, gig-wear, mic) **in your carry-on**. And write your name and email on the shell of your suitcase in Sharpie so it cannot get separated from the bag.—*Tierney Sutton*

Always have a backup of any crucial piece of gear (or music).—*Glenn Kotche*

It's great to look for used musical instruments while exploring new towns and cities.—*David Schwartz*

Pack light. You don't need a new shirt for every day of the week, and you can clean underwear in a sink with Woolite.—*Larry Koonse*

Keep your toiletries and prescription drugs, along with a change of clothes, in your carry-on.—*Perry Dreiman*

Always take earplugs with you, especially if you are on tour with colleagues. Wear them discreetly.—*Pamela Havenith*

Expect the hassles and delays, and roll with it. Travel light.
—*David Arnay*

Looking out the windows of a train through Europe is a pleasure not to be taken for granted.—*Marty Ehrlich*

Always make sure that you are ***not*** in the last row of an aircraft (those seats are against a bulkhead and do not fully recline).—*Jeff Ernstoff*

No travels without aspirin and tissues in your carry-on.—*Claus Hessler*

Be open to other cultures. Eat well and rest. Be mindful and pace yourself.—*Marcio Doctor*

Stick with a partner airline to build status because you need the quiet of lounges, the priority boarding because of instruments, free baggage, etc. Sit in a café and meet locals, and learn a few phrases. Go out and absorb their culture, rhythm of life, art.—*John Beasley*

Keep it simple.—*Ethan Iverson*

Take earplugs everywhere. Two types: special molded ones, plus standard foam ones.—*Su-a Lee*

Never eat from street vendors.—*Bob Barry*

Pack light if possible, and always keep an eye on your cymbals.—*Joe LaBarbera*

If you have enough time between connecting flights, get a chair massage. Zero fatigue when finally landing!—*Cecilia Tsan*

Get a window seat so you can sleep.—*Ruth Price*

Whenever you fly, be sure to use the airline's online check-in service as soon as it's available to get your boarding passes in advance.—*Paul Wertico*

Get Global Entry so that you have TSA Pre-Check, sign up for a mileage account on each airline, and get a credit card with points for mileage! Also, if your credit card gets you into a Club Lounge, that's a bonus for free food/drink!—*Alexa Tarantino*

Always try to limit luggage to a carry-on. And when you have to check your gear, get the best travel guitar cases you can afford.—*Mary Chapin Carpenter*

Pack light and get there early.—*Vinnie Colaiuta*

Plan to get to the airport very early.—*Shelly Berg*

Arrive early at the airport so you can be relaxed. Your relaxed attitude and professionalism make everyone else relaxed as well. This is especially important if you are trying to check in a bass. Jedi mind tricks help as well.
—*Kristin Korb*

Try to use one primary airline.—*Bob Breithaupt*

Keep it simple, travel light, and carry your bags on.—*John Riley*

Sleep on the plane...get to where you are going on time, and do the job!
—*Bernard "Pretty" Purdie*

For planes, always carry on any music, and take every remedy that works for you, so you don't get sick. Also, look three times at your seat and in the overhead to not leave anything.—*Maria Schneider*

For travel gigs, if possible, bring a book of easy-to-read charts of your chosen songs for the musicians to read on the gig. This will save a lot of time and help to make the concert go smoothly.—*Paul Vornhagen*

Get extra sleep, limit your drinking, and eat healthy.—*Jeff Dalton*

This is road advice—"Don't eat junk food. Find good restaurants. Eat well." (Bill Byrne—Woody Herman's road manager/5th trumpet)—*Steve Houghton*

While on the road, exercise every day.—*Lynn Helding*

Be vigilant about staying healthy.—*Curt Moore*

Get as much rest as you can. Staying healthy on the road, in body and spirit, is a secondary art form to the music. Even when not sleeping, learn how to rest and put your mind in a lower gear to prepare yourself for the work ahead. Reading works well for me. If I am reasonably well rested, I can deal with everything else. When I am not, everything else is much harder work.—*Doane Perry*

Be on time. Don't hang your laundry outside the hotel window (especially in Tokyo). Expect to carry your bags, no divas need apply.—*Shelby Flint*

Be ready for the unexpected—missing equipment, lack of onstage space, humidity affecting drumheads, health issues, etc.—*Raynor Carroll*

Expect things to not go as planned or desired. Give yourself enough time, whenever possible, to deal with these changes when they occur.—*Brian Andres*

More People Skills Advice

How you relate to other people can make or break your career! Be nice!—*John Ramsay*

Friends and the people who like you will take you further along than anyone who simply works for you.
—*Bob Barry*

Be kind and considerate to everyone.—*Chuck Berghofer*

Try to see the world through other people's eyes. When in Rome, do as the Romans do...as good as you can.—*Claus Hessler*

In working with artists, knowing music is great. Knowing people is better.—*Jeff Levenson*

See and appreciate the positive. Don't let negative energy get you down.—*David Arnay*

Be a model Human Being in all interactions.—*Lynn Helding*

I think a lot of people feel that when they become successful, then they will be optimistic and open to everything. It's really the other way around. The more open, optimistic, and kind you can be, the better chance you have of achieving success. I think we all fall prey to envy and ego at times. I've found I'm at my best when I can leave those feelings out. Whatever musical job I'm doing, I'm trying to be in the head of my employer. Bandleader, director, producer—the goal is the same. Once I figure that out, it makes the playing/ writing so much easier. Listening is a valuable skill with people and in musical situations.—David Schwartz

Always be on time and prepared. Do what the leader wants...it's art, but it's also a job. Be nice and helpful to your bandmates. Do not feel you have to give in to personal advances or pressures from guys. It will happen...you're not obligated to have a personal relationship with anyone you're not really interested in. Respect yourself.—*Ellen Seeling*

Try to be positive and helpful. This always works in theory, but the reality is that sometimes this is very hard to do, depending on the situation. Try anyway.—Grant Geissman

Many of the people in your network will transition to the professional world at the same time as you. Impress them with your talent—more importantly, with your dependability. Don't discount student colleagues who are not the leading players; they may go into the business side of music, perhaps as a musical contractor. How will they remember you?—*Jeff Jarvis*

For dealing with difficult, manipulative, aggressive people, study the techniques in *Pulling Your Own Strings* by Dr. Wayne Dyer. Saved my career.—*Abbie Conant*

Be nice, loving, honest, and understanding, communicate well, and be someone others can count on. Take the high road, and try to find a way to make every situation resolve with a positive outcome.—*Danny Gottlieb*

Very little about most things in the human experience make sense without people. Appreciate the "phenomenon" of the human experience, and incorporate the best parts of it (that) you discover into your profession.—Joe Deal

If you can remain humble, stay open-minded and retain your sense of gratitude, then you will attract like-minded people. And the reverse of that is also true.—*Gordon Goodwin*

Care about the project, even if it's not yours. Be reliable. As a musician/singer/writer, realize you're part of a unique community.—*Shelby Flint*

Ask people questions about themselves. It doesn't have to be intensely personal, but you can always open a door with "what got you into this music?" Once you ask a question, be sure you actually listen to their response.—*Kristin Korb*

Be respectful, considerate, and positive. Offer to help other musicians with heavy gear to set up.—*Paul Vornhagen*

Practice meeting people. If you're in a crowded room, try to meet everyone there. And be nice! —*Jeff Dalton*

Never under- or over-sell yourself. Be professional. Be nice.—*Brian Andres*

It's held me in good stead throughout my life to keep in mind that at any given moment, someone, somewhere, thinks that I'm a jerk. Everybody is considered a jerk by somebody. So my advice would simply be: try not to be a jerk.—Fred Simon

There are times when musicians don't agree with each other, become irritated, and possibly alienate those around them. I have tried to live in a way where I can look forward to seeing my friends later in life and share stories of the fun we had on and off the bandstand.—*John L. Worley, Jr*

Always be kind. There's no space for egos or nasty people in music. Be open to suggestions, too. That said, be assertive in your convictions.—*Aaron Serfaty*

The most important people in your life are your nuclear family. It is an art to balance your personal relationships and your professional relationships and obligations. Also try not to be a jerk. If some leader is going to hire musicians to work with, it is unlikely that they will pick the musician who has a reputation for being a jerk. A sideman with an attitude is not only a drag to work with, but they can jeopardize the gig and the reputation of the leader to the concert promoter or the club owner.—*Chris Brubeck*

To the best of my ability in every daily interaction, I've tried to be respectful, kind, and listen to others. It essentially costs you nothing and will probably make you and the recipient feel good. And, it could be an opportunity for growth.—*Doane Perry*

Even if it doesn't come naturally, you *must* get out and meet people in the business. Anyone can become a virtuoso in their own living room, but that doesn't get the word out there!—*Joanne Pearce Martin*

Always try to be kind and generous to people. You never know what they might be going through.
—*Christine Pendrill*

Include human kindness and compassion in your art; long after your music is forgotten, people will remember the way you made them feel.—*Robin Meloy Goldsby*

Yeah. Be exactly like me.—*Kenny Werner*

In Hindsight...

I would have learned more rep while at school studying. In the real working world there's no time for practice, and it gets harder and harder to learn all those pieces you'd like to play.—Janet Paulus

I would never have stopped playing classical music.
—*Catina DeLuna*

Learn to play the drums.—*Charlie Bisharat*

I wish I had had more combo experience in college. As the first woman to graduate from Indiana University with a degree in Jazz Studies (1975), I went through the entire program without any combo experience. It was uncommon for women back then to be included in casual sessions, so I wish the Jazz Department had offered small ensembles in addition to big bands.—*Ellen Seeling*

I would have done more keyboard studies to understand chords better.—Don Shelton

I would like to have been better equipped early on in my career in the "business" side of the music industry. I was unaware of what needed to be done after my first few records were released.—*Andrew Rathbun*

Diversified my skills set sooner—i.e., composing, arranging, engineering, and app development.—*Steve Fidyk*

I wish I had been more open to advice and mentoring when I was younger. It took me a long time to get to the point where I could take help from others.—David Schwartz

I would have liked the chance to study harmony in school.
—*Marcio Doctor*

Practiced more and taken more chances in college.
—*Glenn Kotche*

Practiced more piano in school.—*John Riley*

Career-wise if I had been a bit cooler in the studio interacting with the producer (well known) for my second ECM recording (*Drum Ode*), maybe instead of the dozens of labels I have recorded with, there might've been only one.—*David Liebman*

I should have made more time to practice—both on my instrument and with new technology.—*Dan Carlin*

The great recording session drummers of all time have always had a wonderful tool to improve their groove and swing...because they record a song and then immediately listen very carefully to the playback. It is the best way to learn and improve as a drummer and as a band. I wish I would have recorded more live gigs over the years and listened back after each concert to learn from the recording.—*Gregg Bissonette*

Have learned to play the piano, starting at an early age, as well as play the violin.—*Pamela Havenith*

Work harder to become a better sight-reader.
—*David Arnay*

I would have completed a PhD and tucked it away. Without calculation re: career benefits. Just because...—*Jeff Levenson*

I tried repeatedly to get somewhere on piano, advice given to a non-pianist so many times. I am still trying.—*Marty Ehrlich*

Even though I had several professionals with whom I studied privately, some days I regret not having studied music in college. At the time, I did not fit into academia, and classical composition techniques didn't seem relevant to my sensibilities. I should have learned them anyway.—*Nan Schwartz*

Play/study more piano. (I am a woodwind player.)—*Jeff Ernstoff*

I would have spent more time studying mallet instruments.—*Luis Conte*

I would have learned to play tenor sax and fiddle.—*George S. Clinton*

I would have worried less about playing things perfectly. Jazz is all about human expression and interaction. Sometimes I think I got too serious or academic about it. In school, I wish I would have played more "just for fun" and with less concern for if I was doing things "the right way."—*Alexa Tarantino*

I wish I had practiced more and asked more questions.
—*Benjamin Williams*

I would have taken myself seriously.
Become more proficient as a player.—*Shelby Flint*

While minoring in piano, dance, and voice, I should have stuck to piano studies.—*Hal Blaine*

Taken more composition classes.—*Alyssa Park*

I should have continued playing drums...I stopped studying with Ted Reed when I was 16 and put away the sticks at 21. I was talking to Terry Gibbs recently who is 96 years old, and he mentioned that he quit playing vibes but is still gigging playing drums! At jam sessions, there's always a set of drums onstage...a vibraphone? Ah...no.—*Mike Mainieri*

Spent more time working on piano.—*Bob Breithaupt*

I would not have let limiting assumptions play a major role in decision-making.—*Shelly Berg*

I was predominantly self-taught and learnt a lot on the road, so I would have gone to college to study.—*Chuck Berghofer*

I should have stayed with the program that my teacher (Bob Tilles) envisioned for me, which included learning to play vibes, marimba, and being a complete percussionist. That way I would have a broader knowledge of theory and composition and have the ability to compose music on my own. At the time I felt that it would spread me too thin, and I would not be able to achieve my goal of becoming a master on the level of Gene, Buddy, and Max. That's one of the few things I would have done differently.—*Danny Seraphine*

Taken more college-level courses in performance and theory. I am basically a self-taught musician.
—*Paul Vornhagen*

Practiced and networked more.—*Jeff Dalton*

I would have begun studying West-African music/drumming earlier in my career. I have found it most beneficial to balance the study and performance of classical music with music that is strictly aural.
—*Raynor Carroll*

Meditate more and younger! I would have liked to have been a more stable and supportive sideman but wrestling with growing up had me always exuding a competitive spirit!
—*Rachel Z. Hakim*

I would have learned how to sing and play the piano with better efficiency.—*Brian Andres*

When I was at the Interlochen Arts Academy rehearsing two hours every day in orchestra (and because I was a trombonist counting measures for 80 percent of that time), I wish I was enough of a music nerd to be studying the orchestral score of every piece we played during those rehearsals.—Chris Brubeck

I should have (could have) practiced more during my student days!
—John Tafoya

I felt so happy in my studies and feel happy in my career. I wish I played piano better, and I always wanted to have played a brass instrument.
—Maria Schneider

Studied and mastered solfège.—Dale Hikawa Silverman

Be more serious about the piano and about sight-reading.—Aaron Serfaty

I probably would have paid more attention to the art of jazz improvisation sooner.—Joanne Pearce Martin

Although I've been enormously fortunate in my career, I've often wanted to have spent more time studying...everything. Since 2011, after many years of sidelining this interest, I've finally been able to seriously pursue the study of orchestration, something I wish I had begun in my early twenties.—Doane Perry

I wish I had practiced more and composed more. Translation: Be less lazy.—Rick Kvistad

More Advice to Drummers

Less pressure in your snare drum roll.
Let the ring of the drum and snare response
help you. Don't fight them!—*Bill Platt*

I listen for the drummer to provide an emotional and visceral aspect to the music. Good time is important, but a good feel gives the music wings.
—*John Goldsby*

My best advice to a drummer is to listen to how
the music is telling you it wants to be played.
Probably good advice to any musician.—*Fred Simon*

Since I mostly play flugelhorn on my gigs, please hold back
on the volume if the monitors aren't dialed in.—*John L. Worley, Jr.*

Beat it.—*William Kanengiser*
I'll leave room for you; please return the favor!—*Jeff Dalton*

To young players, I tell them to pay attention to the posture
(especially bottom half of the body) and how to hold the sticks.
From the same point of using or playing with a "stick," I have
recommended some to read golf lesson books.—*Sadao Watanabe*

"Kid, you will always work because you play happy drums; your
drumming makes people feel good!" Bassist Eddie Calhoun (Erroll
Garner, Ahmad Jamal) said that to me after the first set of a gig we
were both playing together back in the 1970s, and those words
have stayed with me my whole life.—*Paul Wertico*

Other musicians hate it when drummers noodle.
It could be the difference in you getting the gig!
In other words, do your practicing before the gig...
unless you're the band leader!—*Danny Seraphine*

Listen, listen, and listen.
Think orchestrally and tonally.—*Shelby Flint*

In big band drumming, listen and lock in with the first trumpet
player. If you're recording with an orchestra and you're wearing
earphones, tell the engineer to put the instruments you're playing
figures with into your phones' mix.—*Joe Porcaro*

In the case of the jazz orchestra, you're not just a time-keeper. You are like
an architect for the music. A big part of your job is to shape the story—
to make everything feel inevitable and to make surprises even more surprising.
—*Maria Schneider*

You are the beating heart of any ensemble. Sometimes that needs
to come to the fore, other times just to be going on in the background.
Be sure you know the difference.—*Christine Pendrill*

Seven Questions, Seven Answers
with Jorge Calandrelli

What's the best advice you've ever received?

When I was 22 years old, playing with my Jazz Trio in an elegant club in Buenos Aires called 676, Astor Piazzolla was already performing as a superstar with his amazing and revolutionary Tango Quintet, and one night he approached me and told me he very much liked my harmonies and jazz style. At that time, I was totally influenced by Bill Evans and other great jazz pianists such as Erroll Gardner and Oscar Peterson. Piazzolla, right after his comment, asked me if I was studying music seriously. I told him that basically I was self-taught and had studied some classical piano when I was younger. He thought for a second and said something like, "Jorge, you *have* to study music for real! You don't want to be playing in night clubs by ear for the rest of your life!"

That said, he told me he was going to call his composer friend Carlos Guastavino to recommend me as a private student. Not long after that conversation, I began studying classical harmony and counterpoint with Guastavino for two years. He was such a fantastic teacher that he built the basis of what would become my harmonic concept for the rest of my life! From there on I kept studying composition with private teachers until I was in my early thirties. That obviously changed my life and helped me become a professional composer, arranger, producer, conductor, and pianist—which I now realize was my real destiny!

Going back to the question: to study music seriously was the best advice I've ever received.

What's the best advice you've ever given?

The best advice I've ever given to young musicians is: follow your dream; travel, see the world; be the absolute best you can be; do your next project better than the one you did before; listen to the greatest composers who ever lived, from Bach to Stravinsky to Chopin and Ravel, et al.; analyze scores of classical music (Mozart to Beethoven), and **study, study, study**!

What's the one thing you would have done differently in your studies or career?

I would have liked to concentrate more in music than in having fun while doing it! However, I am not sure that that would have been any better in the long run. After all, we are a consequence of our life, and everything we do has a meaning and a purpose—maybe to change any of those factors would have been like going back in a time machine to change events before they happen!

Best travel advice?

In troubled times like the world is going through nowadays, although it might sound very practical, my strong advice would be: be aware of your surroundings at all times; drink only bottled water; be very careful with what you eat; make sure to always be with a local who knows the place, and don't ever lose sight of your passport, credit cards, cell phone, money, etc.

Best sight-reading advice?

Sight-reading is an essential skill in the life of a musician. There are basically two kinds of musicians: the ones who read and the ones who don't. That makes such a big difference that opens up huge horizons in your career. Young Leonard Bernstein got his first conducting job because of his ability to sight-read orchestral scores on the piano. Especially on the piano, sight-reading is a gift like any other. It can be accomplished by working every day incessantly, but there are musicians that have that gift naturally. I had an aunt in my family that was not even aware of her incredible reading skills—you would put in front of her any piece of music such as Bach, Chopin, Ravel, and she would play it perfectly without any mistakes like a computer! In my whole career I have known very few top studio musicians who can really sight-read very well! And those are definitely the most successful ones!

Do you have any advice for a musician?

If you are a composer, songwriter, or arranger, protect your copyright and your publishing at all costs. Join the unions or organizations that protect you such as AFM, ASCAP, ASMAC, etc. and make sure to make clear deals regarding your fees and conditions. Be very strict with your appointments—make sure to leave with enough time to make it on time. If you say you are going to call somebody, call them. If you have a deadline, deliver everything on time, and so on and so forth! Like a famous executive of a record company once said: "In show business you don't get what you deserve—you get what you negotiate!"

Any advice relating to people skills?

In my experience everything you learn in life has an impact on your professional relations and career. Playing tennis, golf, chess, and being well read, educated, cultured, informed, as well as well groomed might make a huge difference in your human relations. Learning languages is of utmost importance—the more languages you speak and understand, the better your chances are of having an international career. Following up is also very important. When you make contact with somebody who is interested in you, keep in touch (without being obnoxious)— because if you disappear, chances are you'll never hear from that person again! Also, it is important to document the things you do with well-produced demos or recordings and credits that you can show to potential clients. Although the music career is a business, the most important thing is to be musically great at what you do—that's what's really going to determine the level of success you will be able to accomplish throughout the years.

More Words of Advice
from Composer Charles Bernstein

(reprinted here with his kind permission)

Remember the moral of Aesop's fable "The Fox and the Goat": "Never trust the advice of a man in difficulties."

Hank Mancini's sage reminder to "always take partners," meaning, make sure that the producer and director are a party to whatever direction your score is taking.

My old teacher Roy Harris once confounded me by saying, "Just remember, Charles, the notes don't matter." What?! A teacher of composition saying that the notes don't matter? Of course, I asked him what he meant by that. He simply said, "You can change the notes around." Use different notes. It doesn't really matter. Don't hold onto them so possessively. Let it flow. The music can still make its point with different notes. Now that is advice! It can resonate through your whole life. It was his way of saying, "Loosen up, we're not chiseling in stone; it's not the notes that matter—it's the music."

Master ethnic musician Omar Faruk Teklibek was lamenting how he used to overblow when playing a regional flute. It affected his sound, intonation, and especially his stability at the ending of phrases. He concluded that blowing with less force produced a better, truer, stronger result. So, he offered the simple advice, "Don't blow any harder than necessary." High energy is tempting because it may seem beneficial at first. But every process has an optimal level of "wind" needed to propel it. Whenever we exceed this level, we get diminishing returns, distortion, and waste. Isn't this even truer in life?

Teklibek also advised, "...don't think about the next note; there is no next note." **There is no next note.** In other words, you can't invest your energy into a note that you are not yet playing. If you are thinking about some imaginary "next note," then you are neglecting the actual note you are creating now. It's a beautiful way of saying, "Be fully in the moment. Now is all there is. Give this one your all."

© Charles Bernstein, 2001

Our Contributors

Carl Allen: jazz drummer, educator

Brian Andres: drummer, educator

David Arnay: jazz pianist, composer, educator at University of Southern California

Kenny Aronoff: live and studio rock drummer, author

Rosa Avila: drummer

Jim Babor: percussionist, Los Angeles Philharmonic, educator at University of Southern California

Jennifer Barnes: vocalist, arranger, educator at University of North Texas

Bob Barry: (jazz) photographer

John Beasley: jazz pianist, studio musician, composer, music director

John Beck: percussionist, educator (Eastman School of Music, now retired)

Bob Becker: xylophone virtuoso, percussionist, composer

Shelly Berg: jazz pianist, dean of Frost Music School at University of Miami

Chuck Berghofer: jazz bassist, studio musician

Julie Berghofer: harpist

Charles Bernstein: film composer

Ignacio Berroa: Cuban drummer, educator, author

Charlie Bisharat: violinist, studio musician

Gregg Bissonette: drummer, author, voice-over actor

Hal Blaine: legendary studio drummer (Wrecking Crew fame)

Bob Breithaupt: drummer, percussionist, educator at Capital University

Bruce Broughton: composer, EMMY

Chris Brubeck: bassist, bass trombonist, composer

Gary Burton: vibes player, educator (Berklee College of Music, now retired), GRAMMY

Jorge Calandrelli: composer, arranger, GRAMMY

Dan Carlin: award-winning engineer, educator at University of Southern California

Terri Lyne Carrington: drummer, educator at Berklee College of Music, GRAMMY

Ed Carroll: trumpeter, educator at California Institute of the Arts

Raynor Carroll: percussionist (retired, Los Angeles Philharmonic), educator at UCLA

Mary Chapin Carpenter: singer, songwriter, GRAMMY

Gloria Cheng: contemporary classical music pianist, GRAMMY

John Clayton: jazz bassist, bandleader, educator, GRAMMY

George S. Clinton: film composer (*Wild Things, Austin Powers*)

Vinnie Colaiuta: live and studio drummer

Abbie Conant: trombonist (Munich Philharmonic, retired), educator

Luis Conte: Cuban percussionist, live and studio

Marc Copland: jazz pianist, composer, educator

Joe Corsello: jazz drummer, retired police detective

Bill Cunliffe: jazz pianist, arranger, composer, educator, GRAMMY

Jeff Dalton: bassist

John Daversa: trumpet/composer/arranger, professor at University of Miami, GRAMMY

Jae Deal: composer, producer, educator at University of Southern California

John DeChristopher: retired VP at Zildjian, manager

Catina DeLuna: Brazilian vocalist

Justin DiCioccio: educator (Manhattan School of Music, retired)

Marcio Doctor: percussionist, composer, educator

Perry Dreiman: percussionist, Los Angeles Philharmonic

Rick Drumm: retired music executive at D'Addario, consultant

Kait Dunton: singer

Nathan East: live and studio bassist

Marty Ehrlich: woodwind artist, composer, educator

Jeff Ernstoff: woodwind artist, motivational speaker

Damian Erskine: bassist, author, educator

Russ Ferrante: pianist, composer, educator at
 University of Southern California, GRAMMY

Steve Fidyk: jazz drummer, educator at Temple University

Shelby Flint: vocalist, songwriter

Antonio García: educator

George Garzone: jazz saxophonist, composer, educator at
 Berklee College of Music

Grant Geissman: live and studio guitarist, author

John Goldsby: bassist (WDR Big Band), author, educator

Robin Meloy Goldsby: pianist, author

Scott Goodman: drummer, business executive (Zoom North America)

Gordon Goodwin: pianist, educator, composer, arranger, GRAMMY, EMMY

Danny Gottlieb: drummer, author, educator

Skip Hadden: former Weather Report drummer, educator at
 Berklee College of Music

Alan Hall: drummer

Ivan Hampden, Jr.: jazz, R&B drummer

Matt Harris: pianist, educator at California State University, Northridge

Russell Hartenberger: percussionist, educator, co-founder of NEXUS

Pamela Havenith: violist (Bonn Beethovenhalle Orchestra, retired)

Lynn Helding: vocalist, educator at University of Southern California

Claus Hessler: drummer, author, educator

Dale Hikawa Silverman: co-principal violist, Los Angeles Philharmonic

Anne Hills: singer, songwriter, therapist

Gary Hobbs: drummer, educator

Steve Houghton: drummer, author, educator at Indiana University

Matt Howard: principal percussionist, Los Angeles Philharmonic

Ralph Humphrey: drummer, author, educator

Tim Ishii: saxophonist, educator at University of Texas at Arlington

Ethan Iverson: pianist, author, educator

Jeff Jarvis: saxophonist, educator at California State University, Long Beach

Ingrid Jensen: trumpeter, educator

Judith Johanson: principal flute, Filarmonica de la Ciudad de Mexico

Bill Kanengiser: classical guitarist, educator at
    University of Southern California

Jim Keltner: legendary studio drummer

Steve Khan: guitarist, composer, producer

Tim Kobza: guitarist, educator at University of Southern California

Larry Koonse: guitarist, educator at California Institute of the Arts

Kristin Korb: bassist, vocalist

Glenn Kotche: drummer (Wilco)

Rick Kvistad: principal percussionist, San Francisco Opera Orchestra

Joe LaBarbera: jazz drummer, educator at
    California Institute of the Arts

Su-a Lee: co-principal cellist, Scottish Chamber Orchestra

Will Lee: live and studio bass player, GRAMMY

Jeff Levenson: jazz advocate (Hancock Institute, N.A.R.A.S.)

David Liebman: jazz saxophonist, author, educator

Joe Lovano: jazz saxophonist, composer, bandleader, GRAMMY

Kevin Lyman: rock manager, producer, educator at
    University of Southern California

Mike Mainieri: jazz vibraphonist, founder of Steps Ahead, composer

Michelle Makarski: violinist, ECM Records solo artist

Brian Malouf: producer, educator at University of Southern California

Bart Marantz: jazz advocate, educator

Rita Marcotulli: jazz pianist, composer

Christian McBride: jazz bassist, bandleader, music director, GRAMMY

Allison Miller: drummer

Bob Mintzer: jazz saxophonist, leader, chair of jazz department at University of Southern California, GRAMMY

Curt Moore: drummer, educator

Gary Motley: jazz pianist, educator at Emory University

Andy Newmark: live and studio drummer

Adam Nussbaum: jazz drummer, educator

Makoto Ozone: jazz and classical pianist, bandleader

Marty Panzer: lyricist, songwriter

Alyssa Park: violinist (live and studio)

Alan Pasqua: jazz pianist, composer, educator at University of Southern California

Janet Paulus: principal harpist, Philharmonic Orchestra of the UNAM, educator

Jim Payne: drummer, author, educator

Joanne Pearce Martin: pianist, Los Angeles Philharmonic

Christine Pendrill: English horn, London Symphony Orchestra

Neil Percy: principal percussionist, London Symphony, educator

Joe Pereira: timpanist, Los Angeles Philharmonic, educator at University of Southern California

Doane Perry: drummer (Jethro Tull), educator

Bill Platt: percussionist (Cincinnati Symphony Orchestra, retired), educator

Joe Porcaro: jazz drummer, studio percussionist

Ruth Price: jazz singer, advocate, concert promoter

Bernard "Pretty" Purdie: legendary studio drummer

Chuck Rainey: legendary studio bassist

Satnam Ramgotra: percussionist

John Ramsay: drummer, educator at Berklee College of Music

Tom Ranier: live and studio pianist

Andrew Rathbun: saxophonist, educator

Jake Reed: jazz drummer, author, educator

Emil Richards: legendary studio percussionist

John Riley: drummer, author, educator at Manhattan School of Music

John Robinson: studio and live drummer

Otmaro Ruíz: pianist, educator

Lalo Schifrin: television and film composer, pianist, GRAMMY, OSCAR

Maria Schneider: composer, arranger, bandleader, GRAMMY

David Schwartz: television and film composer, bassist

Nan Schwartz: arranger and composer, GRAMMY

John Scofield: guitarist, composer, bandleader, GRAMMY

Ellen Seeling: trumpeter, advocate

Danny Seraphine: founding member of Chicago, drummer

Aaron Serfaty: drummer, percussionist, educator at University of Southern California

Brian Shaw: trumpeter, educator at Louisiana State University

Don Shelton: vocalist (The Singers Unlimited), woodwind artist

Janis Siegel: vocalist (The Manhattan Transfer), GRAMMY

Fred Simon: pianist

Leland Sklar: live and studio bassist

Steve Smith: drummer (all styles), author, educator

Ed Soph: jazz drummer, educator (University of North Texas, retired)

Marvin Stamm: live and studio trumpeter

Tierney Sutton: jazz vocalist, bandleader

John Tafoya: timpanist (National Symphony Orchestra, (retired) educator at Indiana University

Alexa Tarantino: saxophonist, educator

Denny Tedesco: film producer

Cecilia Tsan: live and studio cellist

Paul Vornhagen: jazz saxophonist, flutist, vocalist

Cuong Vu: trumpeter, educator

Sadao Watanabe: saxophonist, composer, bandleader

Kenny Werner: jazz pianist, composer, author (*Effortless Mastery*)

Paul Wertico: drummer, educator, GRAMMY

Tim Weston: guitarist

Jiggs Whigham: trombonist, educator

Liesl Whitaker: lead trumpet, U.S. Army Jazz Ambassadors, educator

Benjamin Williams: bassist

Matt Wilson: jazz drummer, educator

John L. Worley, Jr.: trumpeter, educator

Rachel Z. Hakim: keyboard player, educator

Glossary of Words You Should Know

accent (>): Play the note with a strong attack (relative to the current dynamic level; see *sfz* (*sforzando*).

attack: The manner in which a sound begins.

balance: Occurs when performers adjust their volume so all players in the ensemble can be heard.

b-flat: Anything that is plain or unremarkable, as in "That was a pretty Bb sandwich."

busy: When you're playing too much, you're playing "busy."

cases: Used to store and/or transport your instrument.

clave: The Spanish word for "key" or "clue," and the rhythmic map or compass for most Afro-Cuban and Afro-Cuban influenced music. 3–2 ("Bo Diddley" beat) and 2–3 ("Peanut Vendor") denote the accent scheme over two bars of music (a song will start on one or the other). Listen to the melody, and it will guide you as to which direction the music should be played.

competing thrills: Playing for the audience, yourself, or the music?

crisp sound: Sharp, clean, and clear.

dance: What the music should do.

dark sound: Possessing depth and richness. Not as bright as a bright sound, to state the obvious.

decay: The gradual fading out of a sound.

desky: The sound or impression of a mix move that sounds artificial (i.e., done by means of a move on the mixing board or "desk"). As in, "That sounds pretty desky."

dynamics: Varying degrees of volume.

explosive sound: Giant and sudden.

fat (or "phat"): The feel of a groove that sits deep in the pocket of the beat.

fatter attack: Full and rich. And, generally, placed on the back side of the beat.

four free (or eight free): In the studio, the number of clicks you'll hear before the first measure of music.

free: To play outside agreed-upon boundaries, whether rhythmic, harmonic, or stylistic. Also, as in lunch.

horizontal: A *legato* manner of playing time and comping, generally more swinging than "vertical" (see *vertical*).

improvisation: Creating music as you play. Instant composition.

miscellaneous: Music-making that is unfocused, as in, "Man, that musician is playing some really miscellaneous stuff..."

muted: Softened or muffled.

open: When the length of a section or solo is indeterminate.

ostinato: An accompaniment pattern that is repeated.

phrase: A musical statement or idea.

pitch: The frequency of a note in terms of its highness or lowness.

pocket: Deep time, in which the music is sitting in the beat and not feeling hurried or rushed.

punch: With a quick, sudden blow or attack.

resonance: A ringing or long decay.

ring: A resonant tone.

schmutz: A slight *rallentando* (*rit.*, *ritardando*) or spreading of the beat prior to the final chord of a piece or section of music. As in, "Would you like me to put a little schmutz in before that last chord?"

sforzando (sfz): A sudden, strong accent.

straight eighths: Regular subdivisions that are counted and felt vertically, or up-and-down.

swung eighths: *Legato* and lilting eighth notes with an accent or emphasis on the off-beat; there can be a suggestion or outright playing of the triplet feel (often times, tempo dependent).

timbre: Tone color or quality.

tuning: Changing or adjusting an instrument to sound at a specific pitch.

vertical: A choppy, up-and-down manner of playing time and comping, generally straight eighth in feel, and not as *legato* or swinging as horizontal (see *horizontal*).

vonce: A jazz slang word that can mean almost anything.

Recommended Books

Modern Reading Text in $\frac{4}{4}$ by Louie Bellson and Gil Breines
(Alfred Music)

Time Awareness for All Musicians by Peter Erskine
(Alfred Music)

Effortless Mastery by Kenny Werner
(Jamey Aebersold Publications)

Self-Portrait of a Jazz Artist by David Liebman
(Caris Music Services)

No Beethoven by Peter Erskine
(Alfred Music)

The Drummer's Lifeline by Peter Erskine and Dave Black
(Alfred Music)

Essential Dictionary of Orchestration by Dave Black and Tom Gerou
(Alfred Music)

Music Publishing by Steve Winogradsky
(Alfred Music)

Copyright Handbook by Pam Phillips and Andrew Surmani
(Alfred Music)

Careers Through Music by Chris Sampson
(GRAMMY Museum Foundation/Distributed by Alfred Music)

Additional Quotes

If you don't make mistakes, you aren't really trying.—*Coleman Hawkins*

In fifteen seconds, the difference between composition and improvisation is that in composition you have all the time you want to decide what to say in fifteen seconds, while in improvisation you have fifteen seconds.—*Steve Lacy*

To achieve great things, two things are needed; a plan, and not quite enough time.—*Leonard Bernstein*

If a literary man puts together two words about music, one of them will be wrong.—*Aaron Copland*

I haven't understood a bar of music in my life, but I have felt it.—*Igor Stravinsky*

Musicians don't retire; they stop when there's no more music in them.—*Louis Armstrong*

People won't remember what you said or what you did, they will remember how you made them feel.—*Maya Angelou*

Competitions are for horses, not artists.—*Béla Bartok*

Information is not knowledge. Knowledge is not wisdom. Wisdom is not truth. Truth is not beauty. Beauty is not love. Love is not music. Music is **the best**.—*Frank Zappa*

I chose and my world was shaken. So what? The choice may have been mistaken; the choosing was not. You have to move on.—*Stephen Sondheim*

I take a simple view of life: keep your eyes open and get on with it.—*Laurence Olivier*

Imagination is more important than knowledge.—*Albert Einstein*

Music is the healing force of the universe.—*Albert Ayler*

Advice is what we ask for when we already know the answer but wish we didn't.—*Erica Jong*